Clever Cleaning

Purdy
&Figg

Clever Cleaning

The natural way to clean everything

Purdy Rubin &
Charlotte Figg

NEW RIVER

To our long-suffering husbands,
Stephen and Christopher, who have provided
us with a steady stream of stains.

Contents

HOW IT ALL STARTED

Our lives were changed for ever by one tiny blue glass bottle of hand sanitiser a few months before the Covid pandemic arrived.

We are two great friends who spent years sharing dog walks and school runs. With our youngest children going off to university, we had started mulling over the idea of setting up a small business together. We shared a passion for protecting the environment and trying to minimise the harsh chemical cleaning products in our homes. And one of the things that drove us absolutely crazy was the rows and rows of toxic plastic bottles languishing in the cupboard under our kitchen sinks.

Thinking we could do better, we started playing around in the back of Purdy's garage with different plant-based ingredients. Soon, our experiments came to fruition, and we were creating scented natural soaps, powders and scrubs and even running 'Make your own natural cleaning products' workshops.

Then, in November 2019, three well-travelled friends from Thailand came along to one of the workshops. They mentioned fears about the rise of airborne viruses such as SARS, and asked if we could create a handbag-sized, airplane-compliant bottle of disinfectant hand sanitiser that they could spray on the fold-down tables during their flight home. We made up three small glass bottles using rubbing alcohol, witch hazel and a few drops of essential oil, and they were delighted.

Within weeks, the virulent strain we now know as Covid-19 was beginning to spread across the world. And that was also precisely the moment we were contacted by the owner of the Notting Hill Bookshop. Thanks to the 1999 rom-com, *Notting Hill*, the shop had become an iconic tourist spot for travellers, especially from East Asia. He had heard about our natural hand sanitiser and wanted to know if we could supply him with 500 bottles by the following morning. We were completely overwhelmed, but we roped in Purdy's sons, Charlie and Jack, and worked through the night to make sure that the first delivery would be ready on time.

It wasn't long before the pharmacy down the road was asking if we could supply them with hand sanitiser as well, and we realised we were on to something. This was just the impetus we needed to get our dreams of creating a company making and selling natural cleaning products off the ground. Charlie and Jack, who had always wanted to set up a business together, both left their jobs to jump in as co-CEOs, and we teamed up with a chemist, Anna Slastanova, to develop a range of natural, gorgeously scented and refillable cleaning products that we hoped would stand up against the big guns.

Our hero product, a natural multi-surface cleaner blended with pure essential oils, called Counter Clean, was launched in autumn 2021 and we haven't looked back. Purdy & Figg was ranked third in *The Sunday Times* 2025 list of the UK's 100 fastest-growing private companies, with central London offices and a factory making the products that are much loved by our very happy subscribers. It's been a whirlwind. But throughout all the excitement, we have never lost sight of the mission we had talked about from day one: to create a guide to cleaning and stain removal using natural ingredients. And here it is.

Setting up a business because of our shared frustration with the cabinet of doom in our kitchens might sound a bit random. But in many ways, we had been gearing up for it for years. Charlotte was working at the time as a marketing consultant but with a keen interest in horticulture and essential oils. Purdy had trained in homeopathy, was working as a nurse in the NHS and was a fierce exponent of natural remedies. Purdy's obsession was the harsh chemicals many of our cleaners contained, and what they might be doing to our health; Charlotte was focused on the planet and the way her recycling bin kept filling up with plastic trigger bottles so quickly, even after her children had left home.

And, while we had huge fun in those early days in the garage, playing with natural cleaning recipes and running the workshops with friends, there was a serious side too. The workshops provided the perfect opportunity for market research, and we did a lot of listening. We also went on several courses ourselves, learning about everything from soap making to essential-oil blending. We quizzed plumbers, washing-machine engineers and 'green' dry cleaners, mining their experience in the field for precious nuggets, tips and advice. We studied the latest science about antibacterials and health, and we quickly learnt what people did and didn't want. Our aim, quite literally, was to provide simple solutions that could take the irritations out of cleaning and make it a joy and pleasure, and we soon realised that instead of all those bottles and sprays, we needed only four home-made products to clean the house from top to bottom: a natural multi-surface spray, a window, mirror and glass cleaner, a gentle abrasive scrub paste and a loo cleaner.

With this book we want to share our knowledge, gained over years of trialling ingredients and methods. We will show the potential upsides of forsaking harsh cleaning ingredients and reveal the impressive and versatile powers of natural ones. In the following chapters, you'll learn why we have so many reservations about conventional cleaning products. We will tell you about the seven hero ingredients you really need, and we'll get you mixing, stirring and shaking up your own range of natural pastes and sprays. We'll equip you with the knowledge to tackle almost every possible stain, smear and unwelcome insect invader, while encouraging you to make your home smell like a spa. We are also on a mission to address modern, everyday concerns about sustainability, microplastics and the environment, health, immunity, antibiotic resistance and allergies, and to suggest alternatives to conventional cleaning products that are affordable and that offer savings in both time and space. We believe that using non-toxic natural cleaners is essential to leading a healthy life; and we want to help reduce the mountains of plastic – in our bodies, in our homes and on the planet.

WHAT KIND OF CLEANER ARE YOU?

Have you ever wondered where you sit on the cleaning spectrum? Are you a blitzer, a spritzer or an ever-so-casual feather duster? Try our (light-hearted) quiz and find out.

1. *How often do you clean your home?*
   A. I blitz whenever I see a speck of dust on my floor.
   B. Once a week, give or take.
   C. When I can no longer see out of the windows.

2. *What does your home look like?*
   A. I'm hoping to audition for my own TV reality cleaning show. I know I'm in with a chance.
   B. It's comfortable, comforting and reasonably clean, without being immaculate.
   C. Think Miss Havisham; the cobwebs are romantic, and we all know dust is healthy...

3. *Describe your cleaning style.*
   A. I'm a whirlwind: snapped-on rubber gloves, pinny tied on, bucket, mop and lots of bleach.
   B. Earpods in and multi-surface spray at the ready. Let's do this.
   C. Sitting in an armchair waving a feather duster in the air.

4. What kind of products do you use?

    A. The stronger the better, and gallons of them.
    B. I try to use eco-friendly products but occasionally slip.
    C. I don't need them. My house cleans itself.

5. When you're cleaning, you're most likely to listen to:

    A. My customised deep house playlist on a loop.
    B. Anything with an uplifting vibe to get me moving.
    C. Beethoven's 'Moonlight Sonata'. It's so relaxing.

6. The idea of switching to natural cleaning products is:

    A. Ridiculous. They're expensive and they don't work.
    B. I'm sure they're a good idea, I wish I knew more about them.
    C. Sounds like far too much of a faff.

7. How much do you love cleaning?

    A. I'm considering going pro and just started my own TikTok.
    B. I quite enjoy it, if I can have a cup of tea afterwards.
    C. Is this a joke?

8. Who's your favourite cleanfluencer?

    A. I live for Mrs Hinch.
    B. I don't do social media, but Shirley Conran said it all.
    C. Is that a cleaner with some kind of head cold?

Results

Mostly As: Whoa, you need to read this book before your mop applies for a restraining order.

Mostly Bs: A kindred spirit. Wait, have you already started this book?

Mostly Cs: Mm, I think you should definitely read this book. In fact, you must.

CHAPTER ONE

The Problem with 'Big Clean'

Fling open the doors of that chaotic cupboard you have under the sink in your kitchen and you're likely to find an army of bottles, sprays, foams and creams all screaming 'extra strength' or 'power plus' with frequent use of the word 'max' and smatterings of 'kills 99.9% of germs'. In this post-Covid world, many of us have become germaphobes, and helpless victims of the persuasive charms of 'Big Clean' – the multi-billion-pound household cleaning industry. We confess we were no different. It wasn't so long ago that you'd have found a hodgepodge of bleaches and lavatory gels and umpteen different cleaners for kitchen counters, bathrooms, stove tops, carpets, fabrics, wood, floors, blinds and ovens under our kitchen sinks.

We both had shelves groaning with limescale removers and polishing creams for brass, silver and copper, and then there were all the insect-control products – moth bombs, ant powders, fly sprays and other toxic repellents – not to mention a whole host of sprays for removing every kind of stain imaginable. Some we used on a regular basis, but most were pushed to the back where they languished for years with the holey rubber gloves (permanently attached to a tube of superglue), remnants of old cloths and dried-out plastic sponges.

Purdy has always been a bit of an eco-warrior, and even though she'd worked as a nurse in hospitals, where hygiene is paramount, she suspected she didn't really need most of these products. Many carried toxicity warnings, which made us wonder what kind of impact they might be having on our skin or our lungs. We hated all that difficult-to- recycle plastic packaging, and worried about the potential dangers all those powerful chemicals would present to watery wildlife once we'd flushed them down our drains.

In her iconic *Book of Household Management* published in 1861, Mrs Beeton wrote that perfect order should prevail in your cleaning-products cupboard, as it reflected the order of the house and, by turn, the psychological order of its inhabitants. We had become ashamed of this miserable corner of the kitchen — it most definitely did not suggest perfect order. Something clearly had to change. That's why we set out to discover just how we had become seduced into thinking we needed so many different cleaning products in the first place, and to unpick the possible damage those harsh chemicals might be doing to us.

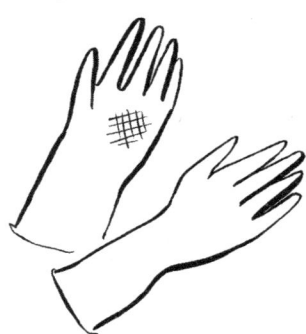

FROM GERM THEORY
TO MR MUSCLE

The boom in household cleaning products began in 1853, when Gladstone finally abolished the soap tax. Up until that point, soap had been considered a luxury item, but now suddenly everyone could afford to use soap to clean their homes and to wash themselves. Manufacturers didn't hesitate to start marketing specialist soap bars. Pears led the way, famously employing celebrities like the Victorian actress and mistress of the Prince of Wales, Lillie Langtry, to endorse the brand.

And then, in 1861, French chemist Louis Pasteur published his 'germ theory', which proved, at the time controversially, that it was the microbes in the air that caused decay, rather than the decaying matter that produced the microbes. It took time for this theory to be accepted, but it eventually launched a hygiene revolution, as manufacturers started to develop not just soap products, but all the disinfectant, antimicrobial, antifungal and antibacterial cleaning products that have held sway ever since.

With the advent of radio, and later television, soap and household cleaning brands found increasingly clever new ways to drive home their message, one of which was the 'soap opera'. In 1927 Colgate-Palmolive launched *The Palmolive Hour*, an American radio concert-variety programme aimed at housewives. It broadcast jazz, show tunes and opera, interspersed with ads for Palmolive – a winning formula that others quickly copied. Ten years later, *The Guiding Light*, a radio show sponsored by soap company Duz, was launched and became so successful that it eventually transitioned to television and remains the longest-running soap opera ever.

Famous Hollywood actresses – esteemed for their good looks and clear skin, as well as their acting skills – began to be hired to promote soap brands. One advertisement had Margaret Lockwood, best known for her role in *The Lady Vanishes*, endorsing Lux soap flakes: 'I make sure that all my pretty clothes are washed frequently in Lux to keep them soft and bright as when they first were new. Only Lux is safe enough to care for my most precious things.'

But it was in the late 1950s, as people increasingly moved away from small grocery stores to shop in large, self-service supermarkets, that household cleaning went truly mass market. Manufacturers started to push the idea of using different products for different tasks: why sell one product when you could convince consumers, who were mostly women, to buy two or three or four?

Before they knew it, women were also being persuaded that they needed an army of strong men to help them around the house.

Mr Sheen, Mr Muscle, Mr Clean, Mr Proper and the unforgettably named Scrub Daddy were just a few among dozens of branded products that came to their rescue – some of which remain bestsellers to this day. All this riled the pioneering feminist, Shirley Conran, who wrote: 'Manufacturers of cleaning products sell them by playing on a woman's chemical ignorance, her feelings of inadequacy, her guilt and her wish for eternal guaranteed happiness and approval. DON'T fall for the ads and DO learn what's in the cleaning products so that you don't duplicate buy.' (From *Down With Superwoman! For Everyone Who Hates Housework*, 1990)

The rise of the cleanfluencer

Despite Shirley Conran's warning, though, 'Big Clean' just kept getting bigger. And in 2020, when Covid struck, we all became obsessed with nuking germs to protect the family. Unilever, which makes Domestos bleach, noted: 'People have more than doubled how often they clean, with 86% changing the way they clean their homes and 66% changing the way they wash their clothes.'[i]

This increase has also spawned the rise of the 'cleanfluencer', some of whom gather millions of followers on Instagram and TikTok by filming themselves whizzing around their immaculate homes spraying, mopping and wiping. Interestingly, at Purdy & Figg, our most popular TikTok posts tend to be the simplest cleaning hacks – like using a cotton-wool pad to clean a toothbrush holder or how to de-gunk your kitchen-sink plughole.

Bacteria have been around for three billion years, well before humanity existed.

Have we reached 'peak' clean?

So here we are, spraying antibacterials on to every surface and glugging neat bleach down our loos in the fervent belief that this chemical barricade will protect us from germs and disease. But will it?

Back in 1989, scientists discovered that households with lots of children and a more relaxed approach to cleanliness had lower incidences of allergies like hay fever. Studies subsequently supported this so-called 'hygiene hypothesis', suggesting that children living, for example, in a rural as opposed to an urban environment, seemed to gain a protective effect from being exposed to a wider variety of bacteria from a young age.[ii]

In the last decade scientists have discovered that vast populations of bacteria, fungi and microbes, which live on, in and around us, could be working on our behalf to optimise our mental and physical health. And that this, our microbiome, does not thrive in the sterile environment created by our over-enthusiastic use of antibacterial cleaning products.

The bugs that live on and in our bodies co-exist with even larger cohorts of microorganisms in our close environment. House dust, for example, contains thousands of bacteria and fungi, and its make-up is influenced by the people and pets who share our homes, as well as other factors such as what we cook and how we clean, and whether we live in the city or the countryside.

The growing concern is that, while antibacterial cleaners may be necessary in specific circumstances, they don't distinguish between beneficial and pathogenic bacteria, and by using a lot of these sorts of products for personal care, laundry and cleaning, we could be routinely taking in too much of a single ingredient that can build up and affect our microbiome and endocrine systems.

There are also increasing fears about the emerging links between antibiotic resistance and the overuse of household cleaning products[iii] because when bacteria are frequently exposed to commonly used antimicrobial cleaning products, they develop crafty mechanisms to survive. Thankfully, the core message of 'nuke everything' is beginning to change as scientists make more discoveries about the importance of maintaining a diverse microbiome and the vital roles microbes play in supporting our overall health.

HOLD THE SPRAY

One way forward is to change the way we clean by targeting particular surfaces rather than blasting everything. A 2019 report by the Royal Society for Public Health[iv] entitled 'Too Clean or Not Too Clean, The Case for Targeted Hygiene in the Home and Everyday Health' suggests that only sites, surfaces and practices that are considered 'high risk for pathogen transmission' should entail the use of antimicrobial cleaning products. Examples of high risk include handling certain types of food such as raw meat, using the loo, cleaning pets and caring for a sick family member who may be shedding infectious microbes into the environment by vomiting or diarrhoea.

What's lurking behind the label?

A friend undertaking IVF treatment mentioned recently that her doctor had suggested she avoid bleach and stick to eco cleaning products. That was when we sat up and began to take notice. Then, another friend being treated for aggressive breast cancer read an article suggesting a potential link between cancer and certain dishwasher tablets. What was going on?

More research is needed on all this, but one study,[v] which analysed 30 everyday household cleaning products, found 530 'volatile organic compounds' (VOCs), including 193 that were potentially hazardous. The researchers warned these 'may cause harmful health effects among professional cleaners as well as among people exposed at home or in their workplaces'. They highlighted cleaning products in spray form to be of particular concern for increasing the risk of asthma and asthma-like symptoms.

In another study,[vi] Norwegian researchers studied the lungs of women who had worked as cleaners or who regularly used cleaning sprays for 20 years. The damage to their lungs was similar to what you'd expect in someone who had smoked a pack of cigarettes a day for 10 to 20 years. These women were also 40% more likely to develop asthma. 'When you think of inhaling small particles from cleaning agents that are meant for cleaning the floor and not your lungs, maybe it is not so surprising after all,' said lead author Øistein Svanes of the University of Bergen, Norway. 'These particles can remain in the air for hours after cleaning and travel deep into the lungs where they can cause infection and ageing of the lungs.'

'Big Clean' may argue that the levels of any chemicals used in their cleaning products are perfectly safe – and to be clear, none of the products on the market today contains toxic levels of any single chemical in themselves – but something doesn't seem quite right. This one is difficult to unpick because the labels on many conventional cleaning products are so bewildering that often only a chemist could decipher what most of them are. Some with long, complex names are harmless, while others may sound harmless but are not.

To further complicate matters, detergent-labelling regulations require that ingredients are listed in a certain way: some compounds are grouped together (such as the non-ionic surfactants used in washing-up liquid and laundry detergents), while others are shown individually (such as the disinfectant benzalkonium chloride, or the preservative benzothiazolinone).

And, although preservatives and disinfectants are listed, it is not easy to monitor our exposure to any one substance. As we have said, no cleaning product currently on the market contains enough of any single chemical to be toxic in itself, but there is a chance of over-exposure if you use several different chemical products that contain the same ingredients together frequently and/or over a prolonged period. It is *the dose that makes the poison*. And, of course, any chemical – even water and oxygen – can be toxic if too much is ingested or absorbed into the body.

The main baddies

QACs *or Quats*

These Quaternary Ammonium Compounds are a group of disinfectants and antimicrobials found in products including bathroom cleaners, all-purpose cleaners and fabric softeners. They will be listed individually on the label as a word ending in '-onium' or '-inium', followed by the words 'chloride' or 'bromide'. The most common is benzalkonium chloride (BAC) used in many disinfectants and sprays, antibacterial wipes and soaps (if a product says it is antibacterial, there's a good chance it will contain BAC). The concern is the way that antibacterial agents like this kill all bacteria – good and bad –

and their widespread use may contribute to strains of bacteria developing resistance.[vii] There are also concerns that when antibacterial substances are rinsed and flushed down the drains, they can damage aquatic wildlife.[viii]

Phthalates

These are often used as stabilisers in the synthetic fragrances found in laundry detergents and air fresheners as well as some plastics. When inhaled or absorbed through the skin, phthalates (and QACs) can become what are known as endocrine-disrupting chemicals (EDCs). This means they can have a disruptive effect on the endocrine (hormonal) system, which controls many of the biological processes in the human body, potentially reducing sperm and increasing the risk of breast cancers.[ix] No label will declare the inclusion of phthalates, but you can avoid them by looking for products that claim to be 'phthalate free' or 'naturally fragranced'. Although individual cleaning products contain very small amounts of EDCs at levels considered to be safe, there is concern that over time as we are exposed to a mixture of different EDCs, they can build up in our body to create a 'cocktail effect'.[x]

Sodium Hypochlorite (chlorine bleach)

This is the broad-spectrum disinfectant found in many household bleaches, bleach-based surface disinfectants and bathroom cleaners. It may appear on the label as 'chlorinated bleaching agents'. It is poisonous for water organisms and gives off highly toxic fumes when it meets ammonia or acids. Never mix chlorine bleach with other products, as doing so can produce toxic gases, which can trigger coughing, nausea, shortness of breath, watery eyes and chest pain.[xi] In extreme cases, these fumes can be fatal.

A manifesto for change

Avoid artificial colours and fragrances

Washing-up liquid is probably the one single cleaning product we use most of, so it's no surprise that it is so heavily marketed and often comes in ever-more garish colours and edible-sounding fragrances. We urge you to ditch the fluorescent pink, fake cherry-scented variety and go for an eco version, by which we mean plant-based, paraben- and phosphate-free, biodegradable, and with no added cheap fragrances or synthetic dyes. We apply the same principles to liquid laundry detergents. There are plenty of eco brands out there to choose from, but we like Ecover Zero Washing-up Liquid and Ecover Laundry Detergent best. We've also noticed a lot of cleaning products emblazoned with green – as in the colour – labels, a fluttering leaf or the outline of a tree, subtly suggesting sustainable or eco credentials, which may or may not be justified. Some products will be packaged in partly recycled plastic and have nothing 'green' in the contents at all.

Think about the waterways

When we rinse out that sponge or mop head under the tap, some of the chemical cleaner we've just used will inevitably rush down the plughole into the drains. It then travels to wastewater treatment facilities, which have various chemical processes and filters designed to screen out nasties and purify the water, so it is ready to be drunk or released into rivers.

Treatment works do a good job of removing many contaminants. However, some chemicals inevitably slip through the net, ending up in our fresh- and saltwater ecosystems, where they can be dangerous to animals, plants and, ultimately, our drinking water and therefore our health.

It is known that the phosphates added to laundry and dishwasher detergent, to soften hard water, can have a fertilising effect, triggering the growth of algae that saps away the water's oxygen, reducing biodiversity. Indeed, domestic cleaning products are estimated to account for one fifth of the phosphates in our wastewater.[xii]

Meanwhile, surfactants (a word abbreviated from 'surface active agents', which are what make many cleaning products foam up and work by reducing water tension), when leached into waterways, can allow plants and animals to absorb other pollutants in the water more easily.

Banish wet wipes

Wet wipes designed to tackle various household cleaning tasks, along with cleaning babies' bottoms, have risen in popularity much to the consternation of sewage companies. No wet wipes of any kind should be flushed down the loo because these sheets are too robust to break down as loo paper does. They gather in the sewers, together with nappies, tampons and other items, attracting congealed cooking fat (which also shouldn't be flushed down the loo or poured into drains) and faecal matter, to form massive agglomerations known as fatbergs.

The largest reported fatberg, according to *The Guinness World Records*, measured 250m (820 ft) long and weighed an estimated 130 tonnes (286,601 lb). It was discovered by inspectors from Thames Water (UK) in a sewage pipe in London's Whitechapel area in September 2017.

Plastics be gone

As well as focusing on the negative impacts of the harsh chemicals in cleaning products, we believe it is important to think about the plastic packaging so many of them come in. There's no doubt that we should all be using less plastic. Relying as it does largely on fossil fuels, plastic production contributes significantly to greenhouse gas emissions. Unfortunately, plastic is seductively cheap to manufacture and versatile in its use, whereas recycled plastic is relatively expensive and less adaptable.

Despite all our environmental concerns, recycling rates around the world are pitifully low. According to the British charity WRAP (Waste and Resources Action Programme), 84.5 million cleaning-product bottles and 126 million aerosols are thrown into rubbish bins every year, when they could be recycled.[xiii] Some of that waste plastic will be incinerated as part of our household rubbish in a process believed to increase greenhouse gasses and create toxic fumes that have been linked to health problems for those living close to the incineration plants.[xiv]

However, any plastic that isn't incinerated or recycled will take hundreds of years to decompose, eventually breaking down into microplastics (smaller than a sesame seed) and then nanoplastics (too small to be seen by the naked eye), which can inadvertently be eaten by fish and wildlife and thereby enter the human food stream.

An estimated 12 million tonnes of plastic enter the oceans annually, much of it from packaging.[xv] One published study[xvi] identified 240,000 tiny pieces of plastic in a one-litre bottle of water. As identification technology improves, researchers have found evidence of plastic particles in human blood, lungs, guts, faeces, placentas and testes. Another recent study found that microplastics and nanoplastics have infiltrated the human brain.[xvii]

The worry is not just the amount of plastic we are unwittingly ingesting through the air, water and food we eat (although it should be said that the potential health effects of these tiny plastic bits are still unproven and unknown), but the possible effect that the chemicals that are bonded with those plastics during their production might have on our bodies.[xviii] These chemicals are thought to interfere with important biological processes and cause disruption to the endocrine and immune systems, affecting mobility, reproduction and development, and even possibly increasing the risk of some cancers.

That's why we are passionate about using fewer plastic products when it comes to household cleaning.

Go natural

Clearly, we should be buying fewer cleaning products and, when we do buy them, focusing on those that use natural ingredients, sustainable packaging and refillable bottles, which are not only healthier and a pleasure to use, but save space, time and money.

Why use all those toxic products when simple ingredients, such as soda crystals or bicarbonate of soda, do the job just as well? And let's not forget good-old elbow grease, as even simple friction on surfaces helps lift bacteria off. In a sense we are coming full circle, embracing the ingredients that were first used for household cleaning hundreds of years ago. In the next chapter, we will show you how.

The largest accumulation of plastic in the world sits in the north-central Pacific Ocean between Hawaii and California. It's called the Great Pacific Garbage Patch and it is estimated to weigh approximately 100,000 tonnes, equivalent to more than 740 Boeing 777s, and growing.[xix]

OUR TEN COMMANDMENTS

When we first started making natural cleaning products, we had not given much thought to the actual process of cleaning: why we do it, how we feel about it or why it has such a low status when the results can be so valuable and satisfying. But we came to realise we'd rather *enjoy* the process than do it resentfully. So, here are our Ten Commandments, which encapsulate our cleaning philosophy based on the psychology of motivation, reward and habit building.

① Begin with the end in mind

Imagine walking through your front door. What matters to you most? Windows you can see through, a clean and empty kitchen sink, a sparkling bathroom, or freshly laundered, crisp sheets on the bed? Or perhaps dust-free bookshelves are your thing. It's up to you to decide how you want your home to look and smell. Don't be swayed by someone else's ideas. There is no set standard of cleanliness; think about your own priorities and, when it comes to cleaning, decide what you're aiming for before you start.

② Three Russian dolls

Imagine a set of three Russian dolls, nestling one inside the other and dependent on each other, The smallest doll is your body, the second your home and the third your environment. For each cleaning task, think about the potential impact a product might have first on you, your family and pets, then on your home and lastly on the world outside. How is the residue from the detergent you used for laundering your sheets affecting the microbes on your skin? How might it affect the atmosphere in your home? Are you okay with what happens to the oven-cleaner waste when you rinse it off your oven racks in the kitchen sink and it travels through the sewage system to potentially enter the water table? And what about the containers these products came in, and where they will end up when you discard them?

3
Little and often

Making the switch from using harsh chemical products to embracing the gentle power of natural minerals requires a whole new cleaning mentality – one that we think is far more congenial in every way. The idea here is to think about cleaning the way you do about brushing your teeth or washing your hair. So, rather than the once-fortnightly massive squirt of bright blue bleach gel around the rim of the loo, try using an eco-friendly loo cleaner two or three times a week – you will banish the limescale and the bacteria that live there, and you will never need to use a corrosive limescale remover again. Similarly, a quick, daily wipe-down of the glass shower screen after your shower will avoid spots forming.

4
Just get started

If you're a natural procrastinator, find ways to get going with a distraction and promise yourself a reward at the end. When we decide to tackle the bathrooms, or scour the hob and oven, we put on our favourite music to keep up momentum and promise ourselves a cup of tea and some chocolate at the end. Apps like OurHome, Tidy and Neatnook are great for helping you organise your time or turning chores into a game with goals and rewards. It's also worth keeping products close to where they are needed: a bottle of white vinegar under the sink, the eco-loo cleaner next to the loo, a bag of oxygen bleach by your washing machine.

5

Make it beautiful

We decided to make our own products partly because so many
eco cleaning products on the market tend to look and smell rather
worthy. We wanted ours to be beautiful and enticing, to create
gorgeous products that would appeal to all the senses, packaged
in tactile glass bottles to be used with the softest cloths and best
brushes. Try to make your cleaning shelf a place of inspiration:
decant ingredients like bicarbonate of soda and white vinegar
into glass bottles and ceramic jars, stick on hand-written labels –
you might even think of buying a labelling machine. The beauty
is in the small details.

6

Embrace new scent memories

Smell is the most primitive and earliest formed of our senses.
When we started our workshops, we'd hear time and again how
people loved the 'clean' smell of wood polish, because it reminded
them of childhood visits to grandparents. Today's young people,
sadly, are likely to have those same memories triggered by a cocktail
of chlorine bleach and cheap, synthetic smells. For us, it's the smell
of natural essential oils that are the most atmospheric and evocative,
which is why we love them. Why not take advantage of their mood-
enhancing powers and start laying down new scent memories?

The secret of sunlight and soaking

Sunlight and a good, long soak in water are two virtually free resources. They have been an established part of laundry routines for centuries but have become overlooked. Sunlight not only dries out and kills bacteria, it is also a natural bleaching agent, especially when used indirectly. Meanwhile, soaking almost anything overnight in water works wonders, from lifting the stain out of a blouse (more on this in Chapter 4) to cleaning a grease-encrusted saucepan.

LET THE SUN SHINE

In her book *Spit and Polish*, Lucy Lethbridge extols the virtues of letting sunshine bleach a stain. However, she also mentions the surprising fact that winter or indirect sunlight is safer and more effective than full sun, which can cause white fabric to turn yellow. Lethbridge describes how grand houses used to have special bleaching lawns in the shade for whitening linens.

Did you Know...

We burn roughly 200 calories per hour doing housework.[xx]

Declutter – a place for everything and everything in its place

Tidying and decluttering are the foundations for making our homes peaceful and pleasurable places to be, as well as easier to keep clean. Clutter is the enemy, so it's worth developing a consistent method to keep it at bay. In the spirit of our third commandment, Little and Often, work through your home, one bag at a time. Whether you're dealing with clothes and shoes, or crockery and nick nacks, it's so much easier to take one small bag of cast-offs to the charity shop than to turn up with all of them in one go. Keep bags handy and aim to weed out what you no longer need as you go through the year.

Be the mosquito

Do you sometimes feel so overwhelmed by the monumental task of trying to save the environment that you just want to give up before you start? If so, remember pioneering businesswoman Anita Roddick's classic words: 'If you think you're too small to have an impact, try going to bed with a mosquito in the room.' We can – and should – be the mosquitoes that make a difference, whether it's to plastic pollution, the spectre of global antibiotic resistance or the rising rate of auto-immune conditions such as allergies. Just think about how many plastic bottles end up in our bins, or the gallons of washing-up liquid and bleach that go down our drains and into the waterways.

How do you eat a whale?

To which the answer is: one teaspoon at a time and don't make the spoon too big. If you're trying to chip away at a mammoth task, the best way is to break it down into its component parts, taking things slowly and steadily. Instead of telling yourself you must clean all the cupboards in the kitchen and put everything back in one morning, set yourself the more realistic task of doing one shelf at a time. Take a break if necessary. This will make everything more manageable. It's also best to finish one job before starting the next one. That way if you get distracted, at least you aren't left with umpteen unfinished jobs around the house.

'I make no secret of the fact that I would rather lie on the sofa than sweep beneath it. But you have to be efficient if you're going to be lazy.'
Shirley Conran, *Superwoman*, 1975

CHAPTER TWO

The Knowledge

When we were holding our natural cleaning workshops, we'd always kick off by heaving a huge box on to the table and then, one-by-one, we'd pull out the dozens of plastic bottles, cans, tubs and aerosols that had once made up our cleaning arsenal and read through the long list of chemical ingredients on their labels, pointing out those that sported scary warnings. It was a powerful way to bang home how we have all been seduced into thinking we need multiple different 'max-strength' products if we're going to be able to clean our homes properly. Then, we'd start leading a kind of cookery course, teaching our willing converts how to make their own simple and natural cleaning products to take home.

Soon it became clear that we were ordering the same seven sustainable, multi-purpose ingredients again and again: oxygen bleach, bicarbonate of soda, rubbing alcohol, liquid Castile soap, citric acid, soda crystals and white vinegar. Whatever household job we threw at them, these compounds — alone or in combination — seemed to work brilliantly. From removing limescale to deodorising pet pee, they were just as effective as all the ingredients in the various products we'd tried in the past, only without all those harsh chemicals and plastic.

Over time, using these seven 'hero' ingredients, we perfected the recipes for four cleaning staples that, as we discovered, were all we needed to properly clean our homes from top to bottom: a natural multi-surface cleaner, a window, mirror and glass cleaner, a gentle abrasive scrub paste and a loo cleaner. These four products now form our core cleaning kit — and we will move on to the recipes for them shortly. But first, a guide to the seven heroes themselves, and their myriad special powers and uses.

THE TOP TEN HOUSEHOLD CHORES WE LOVE TO HATE

(according to a 2023 report on the UK's cleaning habits)[xxi]

1. Ironing clothes

2. Cleaning the oven

3. Full carpet cleaning

4. Blinds/curtain cleaning

5. Dusting

6. Cleaning the back of the toilet, and the area behind it

7. Cleaning skirting boards

8. Cleaning grout/regrouting

9. Vacuuming

10. Washing bedding

THE SEVEN HEROES OF POWERFUL CLEANING

1. OXYGEN BLEACH
STAIN-REMOVER / WHITENER

Oxygen bleach, also known as sodium percarbonate or 'eco or green bleach' has great whitening properties and is a miracle stain remover. Unlike chlorine bleach, it is biodegradable, breaking down into harmless natural components in a few hours. This makes it environmentally friendly and safe for flowing into waterways and septic tanks. It also has the advantage of being odourless. A white powder (a combination of hydrogen peroxide and sodium carbonate, commonly known as soda crystals), it simply dissolves in water to create an active bleach solution for up to 6 hours (before the chemical components safely break down), giving you the opportunity to use it for many jobs during the 6-hour window. Its antibacterial and antifungal properties will kill many strains of mould and mildew. We suggest you use only the 100% sodium percarbonate version (always check the label), which works far better than the weaker versions.

Do:

- Dissolve 2 tablespoons per 1 litre of warm hot water, 40–60°C.
- Use a container with plenty of space as the mixture will fizz up as the oxygen is released.
- Leave the solution to sit for 15 minutes – oxygen bleach takes this long to fully release its gas for maximum stain-removing capability.
- Use within 6 hours.
- Spot test a hidden area for colour safety when stain-removing.
- Rinse the item thoroughly after cleaning.
- Try to buy the 100% version.

Don't:

- Use it on wool or silk, or on porous surfaces, such as marble, granite, limestone, wood and laminate.
- Mix it with soap-based ingredients, such as liquid Castile soap.

OUR NUMBER-ONE HERO

We cannot emphasise enough how versatile oxygen bleach is. Along with being a great whitener and stain remover, it can be used to clean pretty much everything, from greasy pots and pans and tea-stained mugs (no scrubbing needed) to grubby floors and outside decking (see Chapter 2). We start most cleaning tasks with a large bowl or sink full of oxygen-bleach solution. Just remember to read our instructions above on how to mix it with water – boring, but crucial.

2. BICARBONATE OF SODA (BICARB)
SCOURER / DEODORISER

An abundant, food-safe mineral salt with antifungal and antibacterial properties, bicarb has been a star of natural cleaning for hundreds of years. We love to use it as a gentle abrasive cleaner and to neutralise smells. Sometimes you might see it listed as baking soda (in the USA), but don't confuse it with baking powder, a raising agent for cakes. Kept in an airtight container, bicarb will last indefinitely to whiten and scour, but it will lose its deodorising properties over time. To check if yours is still active as a deodoriser, dissolve 1 teaspoon of bicarb in a little vinegar or lemon juice. If it still fizzes, it's good to go. Always keep a note of the best-before date, too.

Do:
- Mix it with water to create a paste for gentle scrubbing.
- Rinse it off surfaces after cleaning.
- Store it in a dry place.
- Test it on a hidden area of fabric (including carpets) first.

Don't:
- Use it on aluminium, wood, brass and soft natural stone as it may scratch.
- Use it with excessive scrubbing.

CHEMICAL TONGUE-TWISTERS

Some of the chemical names for these hero products don't exactly roll off the tongue, so read the labels carefully. Sodium bicarbonate (bicarb), for example, sounds confusingly like sodium percarbonate (oxygen bleach) and sodium carbonate (soda crystals). It is easy to get befuddled about what to use, where and when, especially as some products have multiple uses.

3. LIQUID CASTILE SOAP
MULTI-SURFACE CLEANER

Originally made from olive oil in the Castile region of Spain, liquid Castile soap now tends to be made from a mixture of sunflower oil and coconut oil. We love it because it is made without animal fats or synthetic ingredients, and a little goes a long way. Diluted, it will last between 2 weeks and 2 months, but undiluted it will last up to a year.

Do:
- Mix it with water for general cleaning, washing floors and degreasing surfaces.
- Use it diluted with water to banish insects from house plants.
- Rinse whatever you have used it on afterwards if you live in a hard-water area, as it can leave a soap scum.
- Keep it away from direct sunlight, and hot radiators and pipes.

Don't:
- Mix it with vinegar or lemon juice (it can leave an oily residue).
- Use it on waxed or polished surfaces.

4. CITRIC ACID
DE-SCALER

An acid found in citrus fruits, citric acid is known as 'sour salt' because of its sharp flavour and grainy texture. It has natural disinfectant properties and is mildly antibacterial and antifungal. Its main use as a cleaning agent is as a weak natural acid that reacts with the calcium carbonate in limescale to break it down, so it can be rinsed away. It is useful for descaling just about everything in your bathroom and kitchen. Citric acid will keep for five years unopened, and three once opened.

Do:
- Use it for limescale removal (see page 71).
- Keep it near the loo for little-and-often sprinkles.

Don't:
- Use it on aluminium, enamel, natural stone, quartz and surfaces such as marble that contain calcium carbonate.
- Inhale the powder dust.
- Leave it on surfaces or on the rubber seals of washing machines and other appliances for longer than 10–15 minutes.

Did You Know...

If we derived all our citric acid from lemons, the world's supply of lemons would run out, so most of it comes instead from a type of fungus called *Aspergillus niger*.[xxii]

5. RUBBING ALCOHOL
DISINFECTANT

Used judiciously, rubbing alcohol is a powerful, fast-evaporating disinfectant that kills bacteria, viruses and fungi and leaves no residue, which also makes it a great spot stain remover. It dissolves oils and helps to lift certain stains right out, and is particularly good on chocolate, make-up and ink on items like upholstered surfaces that can't go in the wash. Rubbing alcohol comes in various concentrations, but we always buy s alcohol 70% (often called surgical spirit and marketed for medical use), which is the standard concentration for disinfecting. This strength is the most effective at killing bacteria and viruses, because the water helps the alcohol to penetrate the microbial cell walls more effectively. It works by disrupting the fatty lipid membranes that encase bacterial and some viral molecules and breaking down the proteins inside. It is a brilliant sanitiser in kitchens, bathrooms and high-touch areas, such as light switches and door handles (and makes an excellent hand sanitiser, especially when combined with essential oils). It also works well as a deodoriser – it kills the bacteria that cause bad smells.

Do:

- Do buy the 70% version rather than the 99% version (which can damage surfaces, and evaporates quickly, making it less effective).
- Use it for cleaning and disinfecting.
- Use it as a window cleaner (see page 57).
- Use it as a spot treatment on stains (see page 93).
- Use it to remove the sticky residue from labels.

Don't:

- Use it on wood, painted or varnished surfaces, rubber or porous materials such as marble and some plastic surfaces.
- Inhale the fumes.
- Use it near open flames.

The top cleaning complaints about our other halves are:[xxiii]

- Leaving dirty dishes in the sink (men's complaints about women).
- Leaving clothes and personal possessions lying about (women about men).

6. SODA CRYSTALS
GREASE-BUSTER

Soda crystals – also known as sodium carbonate, washing soda or soda ash – have been used for hundreds of years as a cleaning agent. These crystals are even more alkaline than bicarb and can turn fats and oil into a form of water-soluble soap, which is easy to wash off. Soda crystals cut through grease on anything from oven racks to clothes. They also act as a water softener, removing the hard-water minerals that cause soap scum and limescale build-up. This makes cleaning more efficient and improves the performance of washing and dishwashing machines. A solution of soda crystals made up in hot water will remain active for up to three days. Keep your packet airtight and the shelf life will be three years.

It's best to buy soda crystals from a hardware shop so you can check if the crystals are still soft by giving them a good squeeze. When you come to use them, if they have become hard, break them up with a rolling pin or dissolve them in water, but remember, once dissolved, the solution will be active only for up to three days.

You can also buy soda crystals as a liquid, which is more convenient, but comes in a plastic bottle.

Do:

- Sprinkle them on to surfaces or mix them with a little warm water (40°C plus) to create a thick paste.
- Use them to de-grease ovens and unblock drains (see pages 64 and 80).
- Use them for maintenance of washing machines and dishwashers (see pages 67 and 75).
- Keep them away from hot water pipes and direct sunlight, as any ambient heat risks hardening the crystals.

Don't:

- Use them on aluminium, plated taps, silver or tarnished, polished, painted or lacquered surfaces, as the crystals are caustic and will scratch these.
- Use them on delicate fabrics such as silk or wool.
- Use them on self-cleaning ovens, as these have a specialist coating that will be damaged.

7. WHITE VINEGAR
MULTI-PURPOSE CLEANER / DESCALER

Not to be confused with wine vinegar or any coloured or flavoured vinegars, white vinegar, also known as spirit or distilled vinegar, is more acidic, making it ideal for household cleaning. We recommend 5% acidity (it might say 4–6% on the label), as this tackles most jobs. You'll find it in hardware shops rather than the condiments aisle of a supermarket.

White vinegar is a weak acid with mild antibacterial and antifungal properties that removes limescale via an acid-alkaline reaction that turns it into salt, water and carbon dioxide. It has a potent smell, but that evaporates quickly and you can always add pieces of fragrant citrus fruit peel to your solution, if you really hate it. (We then recommend using the old peel to clean your chopping boards, as the remaining oils in the peel will help cut through grease.)

White vinegar is also a great all-round cleaner and deodoriser, particularly for pet pee because the acetic acid neutralises the ammonia present in urine.

Do:
- Use a 50/50 mix of white vinegar and water for general cleaning and light limescale removal.
- Use it on glass.

Don't:
- Use it on marble, granite, stone, quartz, metal fittings or delicate painted surfaces, as it is quite acidic and can mark them.
- Prolong its use on rubber, such as washing machine seals, again because its acidity can eat into the material.

CITRUS-VINEGAR SPRAY

To make a citrus scented vinegar for cleaning, fill about one third of a large glass jar with any citrus peel, top up with white vinegar, leave to sit for 2–4 weeks, then strain into a spray bottle discarding the peel. This can be used in a number of ways, including combining a spritz of vinegar with a sprinkle of bicarb or soda crystals. Mixing these acid and alkaline substances will dislodge dirt and deposits thanks to the movement of the bubbles. It is important to scrub while the fizzing action lasts as, once it stops, the chemical reaction between the acid vinegar and the alkaline powder is completed and all you are left with is an inactive salty solution.

SHELF LIFE: 6 MONTHS – 1 YEAR

Your hero essentials kit

Now you've got to know the seven hero ingredients, you're ready to tackle every possible household cleaning task – no matter how big or small. We suggest you buy yourself a basic starter kit using the quantities below. Think of it like one of those organic veg boxes with everything you need to get going. This will give you more than a good taste for what's possible and should last for several months, depending on your use. You will soon come to know which heroes you love best and then, we promise you, you'll be ordering them in bulk (in some cases, you will have to choose between heroes, since citric acid and white vinegar, for example, both do some of the same jobs). We stock some of them on our website, clevercleaning.co.uk, as does Amazon, but we also like to support local hardware shops and small ethical suppliers – see Key Suppliers and Products on page 165.

- 1kg oxygen bleach
- 250g citric acid
- 500ml rubbing alcohol
- 1kg soda crystals (or 500ml as liquid)
- 1kg bicarbonate of soda
- 1 litre liquid Castile soap
- 5 litres white vinegar

~~~~~~

MEASUREMENTS
All measurements in our recipes are rounded up or down to the nearest whole number.

1 teaspoon = 5g (a little over ⅙oz)   500g = 18oz
1 tablespoon = 15g (about ½oz)   600ml = 1 pint

The Clever Clean recipes

Although each hero has its own powers, our four Clever Clean recipes combine the heroes in such a way as to cover pretty much every cleaning eventuality. They will simplify your cleaning routine and ensure you're doing your mosquito bit (see page 34) to reduce the quantities of harsh chemicals in your home and on the planet:

1. Multi-surface Spray
2. Window, Mirror and Glass Cleaner
3. Gentle Abrasive Scrub Paste
4. Loo Cleaner

PRECAUTIONS BEFORE YOU START

Even though the seven heroes are natural, sustainable and environmentally friendly, they are not hazard-free. As well as keeping cleaning products away from children and pets, always be mindful of the following safety and storage guidelines to protect everyone and everything in your home.

• Unpack and decant all dry, powdered ingredients into airtight containers to preserve them.

• Keep all containers in a cool, dry spot, away from direct heat and sunlight and out of the reach of children.

• Label everything – and include the date of making.

• Ensure that your pets can leave the room that you intend to clean.

• Wear rubber gloves, especially if you have broken or sensitive skin – we use plastic-free gloves that are compostable and made from Fairtrade rubber (see Key Suppliers and Products, page 165).

• When mixing any powders with water, be careful never to inhale them or splash the liquid into your face, particularly into your eyes.

• Rubbing alcohol is highly flammable so never use it near a naked flame.

• Never mix any of the heroes with chlorine bleach.

Using essential oils

You will see in the recipes that there is an option to include a few drops of different essential oils. Despite their name, essential oils are by no means essential, and if you prefer to make your cleaning products scent-free, they will clean just as well. We both happen to be passionate about essential oils, though – adding them to our cleaning products makes the job so much more enjoyable and we love making our homes smell like natural spas. For the full lowdown on essential oils – what they are, where they come from and how to use them – including their botanical names, plus our recipes for simple blends that are fun and easy to mix, see Chapter 4.

A note on shelf life

We have specified an approximate shelf life for each of our four Clever Clean recipes, but if you notice any changes such as a clear liquid going cloudy, separation into layers, something starting to smell, or a fizzing reaction not happening when it should, discard the batch and make a new one. When using water in a mixture, the shelf life is relatively short because water – even boiled water – contains bacteria.

Multi-surface Spray

This general-purpose cleaning spray was the most popular product we made in our workshops, because it removes grease and grime, smells gorgeous and is safe on most surfaces, apart from aluminium. Use it with a dry cloth to whisk around the house, clearing away dust and grime from the kitchen and bathroom, and leaving a spa-like scent wherever you go.

You will need
250ml just-boiled water
1 teaspoon soda crystals
1½ tablespoons liquid Castile soap

Optional: 20 drops essential oil, such as a blend of sweet orange, pink grapefruit or lavender

Preparation
Pour the hot water into a mixing bowl and add the soda crystals. Stir really well with a metal spoon to dissolve crystals. Combine the liquid Castile soap with the essential oil if using, and add this to the soda crystals solution, stirring thoroughly. Leave to cool before pouring into the spray bottle and labelling.

Usage
Shake well before use, spray then wipe off with a dry cloth. For tougher stains, spray on to the surface and leave on for 1 minute before wiping off with a dry cloth. For polished wooden surfaces, spray on to the cloth and wipe.

MAKES: 280ML
STORAGE: GLASS BOTTLE WITH TRIGGER SPRAY
or re-use an old bottle
SHELF LIFE: 6 WEEKS

Window, Mirror and Glass Cleaner

This is a smear-free, non-streak formula for windows, mirrors, glass (indoors and out) and shower screens that cuts through grime and needs minimal buffing thanks to the alcohol and white vinegar evaporating quickly.

You will need
140ml water
140ml rubbing alcohol
15ml white vinegar

Optional: 10 drops lavender essential oil

Preparation
Mix the water, rubbing alcohol and vinegar in a bowl or jug. Add the essential oil if using, and stir well. Pour the liquid into the bottle and label it clearly, as it contains alcohol.

Usage
Shake well before use, spray on to your windows, mirrors, shower screens or other glass surfaces and buff with a dry cloth.

MAKES: 300ML
STORAGE: GLASS BOTTLE WITH TRIGGER SPRAY
or re-use an old bottle
SHELF LIFE: 2 YEARS

Gentle Abrasive Scrub Paste

Use this concoction for more stubborn tasks — it is a slightly abrasive cleaner for sinks, shower trays, taps, baths and most surfaces, except for those made of soft natural stone and metals like aluminium and brass. It whitens and removes scum, grease and soap deposits. You'll find it a joy to use and will probably finish it well before the best-before date.

You will need

2 tablespoons liquid Castile soap
250g bicarb, plus extra if needed
1–2 tablespoons of cooled boiled water, plus extra if needed

Optional: 20 drops essential oil of choice

Preparation

Pour the liquid Castile soap into a mixing bowl and add the essential oil if using. Stir with a metal spoon, then stir in the bicarb. Add the cooled boiled water half a tablespoon at a time, and mix well until you have a toothpaste consistency. Be careful when adding your water — you don't want the paste to be runny; it should clump up in your hand. You can add a tiny bit more water or bicarb to get the right consistency, if you need to.

Usage

Apply with a damp sponge or soft brush, rub and then rinse off. For tougher dirt and stains, leave for 30 minutes before washing off.

MAKES: 250–300G
STORAGE: WIDE-MOUTHED JAM JAR WITH AN AIRTIGHT LID
(a Kilner jar or similar)
SHELF LIFE: 2 MONTHS

Loo Cleaner

This is our signature recipe for cleaning the loo, which means you will never need or want to pour neat chlorine bleach into it again. This cleaner is not only kinder but, if used regularly, has the added advantage of preventing limescale – which harbours bacteria and which bleach can't remove.

You will need
300g bicarb
200g citric acid

Optional: 30 drops essential oil – for example, 10 drops each of lemon, spearmint and/or lavender

Preparation

Wearing rubber gloves, combine the bicarb and citric acid in a bowl and stir well with a metal spoon. Add the essential oil if using, mix well, and store in a labelled airtight container. The cleaner may harden if you add too much essential oil or if moisture gets into the container, but it will still work.

Usage

Flush the loo first to wet the sides. Using a metal tablespoon, sprinkle 4 tablespoons into the pan and an extra spoonful on to the loo brush to clean under and around the rim. When the powder meets the water, it will start to fizz. Scrub, then flush. Use once or twice a week, both to keep the loo clean and keep the limescale at bay. You can also add a sprinkle of the powder to your loo-brush container to keep the brush deodorised.

MAKES: 500G
STORAGE: AN AIRTIGHT CONTAINER
(such as an old biscuit tin or a Kilner jar)
SHELF LIFE: 6 MONTHS

LET THE SEVEN HEROES
SPRING INTO ACTION

Now you've got our core Clever Clean recipes under your belt, we are going to show you how to get even more from the seven hero ingredients, room by room. You can use them for a whole range of other simple household tasks – from getting baked-on gunge off barbecue racks to deodorising your fridge.

Kitchen

Removing tea and coffee stains in mugs and teapots
BICARBONATE OF SODA / OXYGEN BLEACH

Purdy's husband Steve usually has a cup of black tea welded to his side when he's at home, so for her, finding an easy solution to getting rid of black tea stains became imperative. She discovered that the simplest way to clean tea – and coffee – stains from mugs and teapots is to tip half a teaspoon of oxygen bleach into the mug and top up with warm water to the brim. Leave the mug to soak for a couple of minutes, pour out and rinse. You can reuse the same solution for multiple mugs. For teapots, make a solution using 2 tablespoons of oxygen bleach per 1 litre of hot water (scale up for larger teapots). Avoid using oxygen bleach on ceramics with metallic or delicate, painted designs, as the bleach may cause fading in time.

Alternatively, sprinkle a couple of teaspoons of bicarb into your mug or teapot and gently scrub with a washing up brush or a cloth. Using oxygen bleach saves you the scrubbing.

Cleaning thermoses and water bottles
OXYGEN BLEACH

Pour a solution of 1 teaspoon of oxygen bleach dissolved in 1 litre of hot water into your thermos/water bottle and leave for 20 minutes. Shake, empty and rinse thoroughly.

>> DOUBLE DUTY: You can clean several bottles and any crockery with stains at the same time by re-using the solution within the 6-hour window.

Cleaning hobs, kitchen surfaces and tiles
BICARBONATE OF SODA
Bicarb is great for cleaning most kitchen and bathroom surfaces without scratching, and its gentle abrasive properties are great at tackling oily residues. Make a paste the consistency of toothpaste by mixing a few drops of warm water with bicarb, then dip a cloth into the mixture and scour away. We would recommend going in gently with a sponge on delicate surfaces. Alternatively, sprinkle bicarb on to a clean, damp cloth and wipe down surfaces, then rinse. This works well for sinks, baths and plugholes, but avoid using bicarb on porous stone surfaces, such as marble and granite, and on soft metals.

Cleaning burnt-on food in pots and pans
OXYGEN BLEACH / SODA CRYSTALS
Both oxygen bleach and soda crystals work like a dream. Dissolve 2 tablespoons of oxygen bleach in 1 litre of hot water and leave to soak for 20 minutes. Lightly scrub and you will see the debris start coming away from the sides of the pan immediately. Rinse. Alternatively, for really greasy pans, dissolve 5 tablespoons of soda crystals in 500ml of hot water with a teaspoon of washing-up liquid. If using liquid soda crystals, pour 2 teaspoons of the liquid and 1 teaspoon of washing-up liquid into the pan and add hot water. After 1 hour or so, scrub and the debris should come away. Rinse. Remember, soda crystals can corrode the surface of aluminium pans.

WHAT'S WRONG WITH MY SCOURER?

Not only do metallic and plastic scourers harbour bacteria, they are also an environmental nightmare. Just imagine how many shards of metal and fragments of plastic are being shed into the waterways with every use. We've discovered a range of fantastic eco-scourers called 'cleaning blocks', which we love (see Key Suppliers and Products, page 165). They are small blocks of recycled glass that resemble a pumice stone or a block of volcanic lava full of tiny bubbles. They look like they could damage delicate surfaces, but they are ace at removing stubborn limescale from hard-to-reach places in loos, sinks and basins, and won't scratch. You can also use them to remove encrusted dirt and grease from barbecues, grills and oven trays. Just wet the block and gently scrub away, then wipe off the residue with a wet cloth or rinse with water. You can add a sprinkle of citric acid if you need extra power in the loo. Look after the blocks by rinsing them under running water after use, scrubbing with a little washing-up liquid and if you want to sanitise them, pop them into a strong solution of oxygen bleach (3 tablespoons to 1 litre of water) for up to 1 hour. You will need to weigh the block down with something heavy, otherwise it will float. The blocks last for ages without wearing away.

Cleaning oven and barbecue racks and roasting tins

BICARBONATE OF SODA / SODA CRYSTALS

Oven cleaning is not a pleasant task because the grease and grime can be determinedly baked on and conventional oven cleaners contain caustic chemicals that smell nasty. But our seven heroes make this job easier. First, warm the oven for 5 minutes to soften any baked-on debris (use the interior light or use your mobile phone torch to help you see what you're dealing with). Meanwhile, mix 200g of soda crystals with 100g of bicarb and 2 teaspoons of washing-up liquid in a bowl, then slowly pour in 160ml of just-boiled water to make a paste. Turn the oven off before you start to clean. Wearing rubber gloves, use an old cloth or spatula to apply the paste to the oven interior, racks and baking tins and leave it for 1 hour or overnight. Then, gently scrub with a non-metal scourer to remove the debris. For a more abrasive action, sprinkle some soda crystals on to your cloth and scrub, then rinse with clean water. If you still find tough baked-on areas, use a recycled glass cleaning block for the job (see box, page 63) and rinse with clean water.

 Not recommended for self-cleaning ovens or heating elements.

Eradicating fridge smells

OXYGEN BLEACH / WHITE VINEGAR / BICARB

Your fridge shouldn't smell of anything, but if it does and your freezer compartment is integrated into the fridge, it could taint your ice cubes. We suggest regularly emptying the fridge and wiping off any food debris. Then, using either 1 tablespoon of oxygen bleach to 500ml of hot water or a 50/50 mix of white vinegar and water in a spray bottle, clean the inside of the empty fridge and wipe it dry with a cloth. If smells linger, try putting several tablespoons of bicarb (4 tablespoons for under-the-counter fridges, 6 tablespoons for average-sized free-standers, 8 tablespoons for large) into an empty jar at the back of the fridge with the lid off. We like to leave a small teaspoon in the jar just to remind us to stir it occasionally to refresh the deodorising action. Replace every 4–6 weeks depending on the size of your fridge, how much food is in it and if there is anything particularly pungent, such as stinky cheese.

>> **DOUBLE DUTY:** You can repurpose the discarded bicarb by turning it into a paste: mix it with a little water or sprinkle it on to a damp sponge to scour, whiten and clean kitchen surfaces such as those of your sink, microwave or cooker.

Eradicating kitchen food smells
WHITE VINEGAR
While we love the smell of freshly baked bread, we'd rather not breathe in fumes from burnt toast or fried fish. White vinegar is great for eliminating some of the worst kitchen pongs (it works surprisingly well to neutralise fresh paint smells too, if you leave an open jar of white vinegar in the room overnight). Just heat a pan with a 50/50 mix of white vinegar and water, and add 10 drops of spearmint or lemon essential oil, a few slices of lemon or lemon peel and a few cloves or cinnamon sticks if you have any. Simmer for 30 minutes and let the aroma clear the unwanted smells.

>> **DOUBLE DUTY:** After eliminating your kitchen smells, you can re-purpose the solution as a loo cleaner. Just strain out the lemon, cloves and cinnamon and allow it to cool. Then pour the solution into your loo bowl to help dissolve mineral deposits and remove stains. Leave in the bowl for 30 minutes or more, then scrub the area and flush. Incidentally, coffee grounds, once used, also do a great job of neutralising food odours so long as they are dry, because they absorb moisture. Leave your discarded coffee grounds in an open bowl on your kitchen counter overnight.

THE POWER OF LEMONS – YOUR EXTRA HERO

Lemons are very useful for certain kitchen jobs. They can:

• *Banish microwave smells*
Squeeze the juice of a lemon into a microwave-safe bowl.
Add the lemon halves and 250ml of water, then put the bowl
in the microwave and turn it on at high power for 4–5 minutes.
Leave the door closed for 15 minutes, then remove the bowl
and wipe the microwave clean.

• *Refresh the dishwasher*
Reuse a squeezed lemon half by piercing it on the top rung
of your dishwasher. When you next open it after a wash, you
will find your glasses sparkle and dishes smell of lemons.

• *Clean chopping boards*
For a quick clean, sprinkle your board with coarse salt and
use half a cut lemon to scrub it before rinsing and drying.

Cleaning and disinfecting chopping boards
RUBBING ALCOHOL
To disinfect boards after preparing raw meat or fish, clean your board, then spray on rubbing alcohol and leave it for 5 minutes to kill germs. Rinse with warm water and dry. (See also 'The power of lemons', in the box opposite).

Cleaning and deodorising dustbins
BICARBONATE OF SODA / OXYGEN BLEACH
Wash the inside and outside of your dustbin with a mild solution of oxygen bleach – 1 tablespoon per litre of warm/hot water); and for a quick refresh, sprinkle a few tablespoons of bicarb inside the base when it's dry.

Descaling the kettle
CITRIC ACID
If you live in a hard-water area, your kettle will need regular descaling. Half fill the kettle with water and bring it to the boil. Add 3–4 tablespoons of citric acid, which will make it fizz up. Leave for 20 minutes, then empty. When emptying, leave the solution to sit in the spout for a few seconds. Then, pour some of it on to a clean cloth to wipe the outside of the kettle. Give the kettle a rinse with fresh water and you're good to go.

Refreshing your dishwasher
SODA CRYSTALS / WHITE VINEGAR / CITRIC ACID
If your dishwasher starts to smell, take out the filter, sprinkle some soda crystals on it and scrub, adding a squirt of washing-up liquid, if necessary. Rinse the filter in warm or hot water, then put it back into your machine. Now wipe down the seal with white vinegar (use an

old toothbrush to get into the grooves) and rinse with a clean damp cloth. Pour 1 tablespoon of citric acid into the soap compartment and 7 tablespoons of citric acid on to the floor of the machine and run it on the shortest, hottest wash.

Polishing grubby hard-surface floors
CASTILE SOAP / OXYGEN BLEACH
We like to use a weak solution of liquid Castile soap as a floor cleaner, because it works well and is so gentle: if you've got pets or crawling babies, you don't want them picking up the residue of harsh chemical cleaners through their paws, or hands and knees. Our basic floor-cleaning mixture is: 1 tablespoon of liquid Castile soap to 2 litres of hot water, or 2 tablespoons of liquid Castile soap to the same amount of water for really grubby floors.

For tough spots and a deeper clean, rinse off the liquid Castile soap, then mop with an oxygen bleach solution (3 tablespoons of oxygen bleach to about 5 litres of hot water). If you have any prominent stains, sprinkle a few dampened granules of oxygen bleach directly on to the stain. Leave for 15 minutes, then rub the granules into the stain with a damp cloth and rinse the floor. Avoid using oxygen bleach on waxed or unsealed floors.

Removing sticky adhesive residue
RUBBING ALCOHOL
To get rid of that annoying residue left by glue, say, from a price sticker or shop label, on non-porous surfaces such as glass, metal and certain plastics, spray rubbing alcohol on to a cloth and gently rub until the residue dissolves (avoid excessive pressure to prevent scratching the surface), then wipe with a damp cloth. If needed, rinse with soapy water and dry with a clean cloth. Do not use rubbing alcohol on porous surfaces, painted finishes, lacquered surfaces or acrylic.

Disinfecting surfaces

RUBBING ALCOHOL / WHITE VINEGAR

You don't need an antibacterial or antimicrobial spray cleaner if you've got rubbing alcohol in your cleaning kit. This is a great disinfectant and can be transformed into a scented, multi-purpose spray to use on countertops, bathroom fittings, light switches and doorknobs and is especially useful if someone at home has an infectious bug. Decant it into a spray bottle and add 15 drops of essential oil per 100ml of alcohol. Lemon, geranium or lavender all work well with the smell of the alcohol. Shake well, then spray and leave on surfaces for at least 30–60 seconds to ensure disinfection. Some surfaces, like wood or certain plastics, may not tolerate alcohol well and could be damaged over time. In these cases, a 50/50 mix of white vinegar and water works as a mild disinfectant – although it isn't as effective against viruses and bacteria, and you can't add essential oils as they won't mix with the water.

Unblocking sink pipes and plugholes

SODA CRYSTALS

No need to run to the hardware shop for a bottle of drain unblocker when you've got your seven hero products at home. Here's what to do: first, slowly pour a kettle full of very hot water down the drain to soften the grease and loosen debris. Next pour 200g of soda crystals down the plughole. Leave for 5–15 minutes to allow the crystals to loosen the debris and soften the grease while you re-fill the kettle and put it back on to boil. Carefully trickle another kettle full of hot water down the drain to clear the soda crystals and help break up the fat and grease.

For severe blockages, repeat this process several times. Once you have your drains running freely again, try to keep on top of the situation. We recommend keeping plugholes grease-free and smelling fresh with a monthly maintenance. For this, pour 100g of soda crystals down the plughole, followed by a kettle of hot water. Occasionally, you may need to use a plunger or a drain snake, which is an affordable, flexible plastic tool that removes hair and minor clogs from sinks and shower drains (see Key Suppliers and Products, page 165). And, if you haven't already got one, do invest in a fine-mesh sink strainer to stop hair and food debris going down in the first place. Another tip: when you have surplus oil or grease left in the pan, instead of wiping it out with kitchen paper, you can add enough oats to the grease to soak it up and leave it out for the birds.

Bathroom

Eradicating limescale in your loo
CITRIC ACID

The limescale rim that can appear at the waterline in the bowl of the loo looks nasty and can harbour bacteria. Most people use bleach to get rid of it, but we have discovered a much better approach. Mix a solution of 125g of citric acid with 2–3 litres of hot water and allow it to dissolve. While the solution is cooling slightly – you don't want to crack the pan – take the loo brush and pump the water in the loo round the bend about 10 times to expose the bare limescale – this is important. Now pour the hot citric-acid solution into the loo – and you will see the limescale disappear before your eyes. Leave for 10–30 minutes, then scrub any remaining limescale away with the loo brush or a recycled glass cleaning block (see box on page 63). Be sure to flush when finished to get rid of the unsightly but harmless brown deposits that may settle overnight.

Incidentally, if you have a septic tank, be wary of using more than about 200g of citric acid a month, as it can affect the tank's biome. (Yes, even septic tanks have their own bacteria-rich biomes.) You can alternate using it with white vinegar and bicarb – again, heating the vinegar can make it more effective. Heat 200ml vinegar in a saucepan and leave to cool slightly, then pour it on to the limescale in the loo pan and leave for a couple of minutes. Sprinkle 2 tablespoons of bicarb on top, give it a good scrub then and flush.

Removing limescale and soap scum on the shower head
CITRIC ACID

There's nothing worse than a feeble shower. If the holes in your shower head are clogged with limescale and soap scum, citric acid is the answer. Dissolve 5 tablespoons of citric acid in 2 litres of hot water in a bowl or bucket (you'll need to fully submerge the showerhead). Take the showerhead and submerge it in the solution for 30 minutes, then rinse. If any holes are still clogged, use an old toothbrush to gently scrub away the debris. For fixed showerheads, make a smaller amount of the solution and dip the toothbrush into it. Scrub enthusiastically, then rinse. Alternatively, you can fill an old plastic bag with the cooled acidic solution and tie it around the fixed showerhead to soak it for 30 minutes before scrubbing.

LIMESCALE IS THE ENEMY

Limescale affects over 60% of households in the UK. It forms when water evaporates and leaves residues of calcium, magnesium and iron salts, which build-up over time into a grey, cement-like deposit. This not only clogs up pipes, taps and shower heads, but also dulls chrome surfaces, harbours bacteria and looks horrible. Build-up happens faster on hot surfaces, like the heating elements in kettles, washing machines and dishwashers, as well as inside irons. These then have to work harder to reach the required temperatures, shortening their lifespans and raising electricity costs. You can check online how hard the water is in your area, and use water hardness test strips to gauge the limescale content at home. If you do have hard water, consider installing a water softener or use some of the heroes to soften the water for certain uses. (See page 75 for our tips on laundry softening.)

Sparkling mirrors, glass, shower screens, tiles and windows
RUBBING ALCOHOL / WHITE VINEGAR

Our Clever Clean recipe (see page 52-9) contains rubbing alcohol, white vinegar and water, and it makes the best cleaner for glass and mirrors, but if you don't have rubbing alcohol, a 50/50 mix of white vinegar and water in a spray bottle is a good alternative for making your mirrors sparkle. Lightly spray on to the surface and leave it to sit for a few minutes, which will enhance its effectiveness. Wipe clean and buff with another dry cloth. It's best to clean windows on a cloudy day as direct bright sunshine can cause the white vinegar to dry too quickly, leaving streaks.

Banishing light limescale on taps
WHITE VINEGAR

For light limescale deposits on taps, soak a piece of kitchen paper or a rag in undiluted white vinegar and wrap the paper or rag around the limescale. Leave it on for up to 1 hour, ensuring the vinegar doesn't dry out, then rinse it thoroughly and wipe it dry. You can use vinegar on most taps, including chrome-plated or brass, as long as they are not in contact with the vinegar for more than 1 hour.

! **Do not use white vinegar on nickel-plated taps as it may damage the finish.**

Cleaning grout
OXYGEN BLEACH
Start with making a solution of oxygen bleach. Dissolve 1 tablespoon of oxygen bleach in 250ml of hot water, put your gloves on and apply the warm solution to the grout with a washing-up brush or an old toothbrush. Leave for 30–60 minutes, then rinse with cool water.

For tougher mould and stains, you may need to follow this up with a strong paste (which is also easier to use on horizontal surfaces). Mix 1 tablespoon of oxygen bleach with up to 1 tablespoon of hot water in a small bowl and stir well until it forms a paste. Apply the paste to the grout with a cloth or an old toothbrush and leave for 15–30 minutes, then scrub with an old toothbrush and rinse thoroughly. On vertical surfaces, scrub immediately after application (it won't adhere as well as for horizontal). You should see the mould starting to disappear before your eyes. Leave what's left of the granules on the surface for 15 minutes – stick some damp kitchen paper over the paste to help it adhere, if necessary, then scrub again and rinse. This gets rid of most strains of mould, but be aware that once mould has got under the silicone seal, nothing will get rid of it without dissolving the seal too. That's why it is so important to tackle mould when you first see it – the perfect example of the benefits in our little-and-often approach.

Soaking away mildew on shower curtains
OXYGEN BLEACH
Before the soaking process, test a hidden area for colour fastness. Fill a bucket, sink or bath with hot water and dissolve 2 tablespoons of oxygen bleach per 1 litre of water. Submerge the shower curtain in the solution and leave to soak for up to 6 hours. If there's any extra room add stained tea towels or dishcloths to soak alongside the curtain. Rinse the curtain with water and launder according to the care instructions.

Laundry

Eradicating limescale in washing machines
CITRIC ACID

Aim to descale your machine every 2 months, especially if you live in a hard-water area. You will know it needs doing if you see a chalky white residue on your clothes or your machine is noisier than usual.

Pour 250g of citric acid into the drum of your washing machine and run an empty hot cycle. Use an old toothbrush dipped into citric acid to scrub the detergent dispenser drawer.

Softening laundry
WHITE VINEGAR / SODA CRYSTALS

White vinegar is an excellent natural alternative to fabric softeners because it helps remove soap residue, reducing static and leaving towels absorbent. It also deodorises your machine. Don't worry about the smell, it disappears during the wash. For larger loads, fill the fabric-softener compartment of your dispenser, and for smaller loads use 120ml. Alternatively, add 2 tablespoons of soda crystals directly into the drum before starting a laundry load.

Preventing bacteria and mould build-up in your washing-machine seal
SODA CRYSTALS / WHITE VINEGAR / OXYGEN BLEACH

If you notice your washing machine smells or there's a stale smell on your clothes even after you have washed them, this could be because of mould on your rubber seal and in the soap dispenser. Mould and bacteria love washing machines because they're dark, humid places with little ventilation.

When necessary, deep clean your machine by adding 500g of soda crystals directly into the empty drum and running the hottest wash programme you have (60°C or higher; no need for a pre-wash). As a general rule, it also helps not to add too much detergent to your wash as this creates more suds, which collect not only in your clothes, but in and around the internal parts of your machine, encouraging mould.

If you've got stubborn mould and bacteria on the rubber seal, you can use a 50/50 mix of white vinegar and water for an occasional deep clean. White vinegar is ideal because it kills some mould and bacteria and neutralises odours. However, it is acidic and if used too often, it could degrade the rubber seal. Wearing rubber gloves, fill a bowl with a solution of 500ml each of white vinegar and water, then soak two or three cloths, tea towels or sheets of kitchen paper in it until saturated. Take them out of the solution and roll them into sausage shapes. Line the inside of the seal with these sausages and leave for 30 minutes. After 30 minutes remove the cloth(s) and scrub away the debris with an old toothbrush or washing-up brush.

If the gunk is bad, you will need a more abrasive scrub, so dip the wet brush in a tablespoon of soda crystals and scrub away. Wipe off the debris with a cloth, rinse the seal in fresh water and dry it. If you can still see a black stain, sprinkle 2–3 teaspoons of 100% oxygen bleach on to a damp cloth or kitchen paper and spread it over the area. Leave this for 1 hour, then scrub and rinse the seal with clean water and dry it. Because vinegar is acidic, we recommend alternating these different solutions.

Whitening whites

OXYGEN BLEACH

Oxygen bleach is your friend here. It is colour safe, but if you have any colour on your (predominantly) white garments, always test your chosen solution on a hidden area first. And, if you have sensitive skin, wear gloves. For normal washing-machine loads, add 1 tablespoon of oxygen bleach directly into the drum of your washing machine along with your usual laundry detergent. For full loads or tough stains, add 2 tablespoons of oxygen bleach directly to the drum. For tired-looking whites that need brightening, dissolve 2 tablespoons of oxygen bleach in 3 litres of warm water (30–40°C). Soak the whites for up to 6 hours, then launder as usual.

Deodorising textiles and trainers

RUBBING ALCOHOL

Use rubbing alcohol to disinfect and deodorise trainers, vintage shop finds and post-party clothes that are clean but a bit frowsty. Decant your rubbing alcohol into a small spray bottle and label it. For trainers, spritz two or three times into each shoe. For clothes and textiles, spray lightly and leave to dry in a well-ventilated room.

Some manufacturers now sell machines with black seals that can hide a mould problem. Remember, even if you can't see it, there will be build-up over time. Keep cleaning — little and often.

Upholstery, carpets and drawers

Refreshing musty-smelling cupboards and drawers
BICARBONATE OF SODA

Take a jar and fill it with bicarb. Then take a small piece of muslin or loose-woven cloth and secure it over the the jar with an elastic band. Place it in the offending drawer or cupboard and the bicarb will literally eat up the smell. This should take about 24 hours – although very strong smells may take up to a week. You can also add 6 drops of essential oil – we use lavender.

>> **DOUBLE DUTY:** Refresh the jar every few weeks and use the old bicarb to scour and whiten your loo.

Revitalising carpets and rugs
BICARBONATE OF SODA

With bicarb you have your very own Shake 'n' Vac. Lightly sprinkle a thin layer of bicarb directly on to the carpet or rug. Use approximately 2–3 tablespoons per square metre. Leave for 15–30 minutes – or, for tougher odours, leave to sit overnight, which will allow better absorption. Vacuum thoroughly. See our guide on pages 131–4 for how to get rid of some stains on carpets.

Banishing pet and pet-pee smells

BICARBONATE OF SODA / RUBBING ALCOHOL / WHITE VINEGAR

If your carpet or rug smells doggy, give the area a good sprinkling of bicarb and leave for 2 hours or overnight, before vacuuming. If the smells remain, dip a cloth into a 50/50 mix of white vinegar and warm water, then dab the area but be careful not to soak it. Rinse with warm water and dab dry with a clean cloth. Finally, sprinkle the area again with bicarb and leave for 2 hours, or overnight if possible, before brushing off the excess and vacuuming. This will also deter your pet from revisiting the same area.

Pet beds can become rather stinky, too, as Charlotte found with her dog Fred. If the bed is machine washable, wash it according to the care label, adding 250ml (1 cup) of white vinegar to the wash cycle. Dry it, then once it's dry, take the bed outside and spray with a light mist of rubbing alcohol, but don't wet it. Leave for 5 minutes – the rubbing alcohol will evaporate quickly and disinfect the bed. For non-washable beds, sprinkle bicarb liberally on to the bed, shake and brush off the excess (outside if you can), then leave overnight and vacuum thoroughly, followed by a light spraying of rubbing alcohol.

Outside

Cleaning the decking

OXYGEN BLEACH

We hate the idea of using harsh chemicals in the garden just as much as in the house, and there's absolutely no need when you've got oxygen bleach. It is brilliant at removing dirt, mould and mildew from sealed wood and composite decking. The active ingredients are safe for wildlife and bio-degrade in 6 hours. First, remove leaves, dirt and other debris with a broom or leaf blower. Mix oxygen bleach with hot water (2 tablespoons per litre for moderate cleaning; 4 tablespoons for tougher jobs), then sponge, mop or pour the solution on to the deck, ensuring that the entire surface is covered. Leave to sit for 15 minutes (30 minutes for heavy soiling), and make sure it doesn't dry out. Scrub the deck with a brush to loosen the grime, then rinse with fresh water, ideally using a garden hose. Do not use oxygen bleach on unsealed, painted or stained decking without testing, as the moisture can seep into the wood.

Cleaning outdoor drains

SODA CRYSTALS

Before you start, check your drain for obvious blockages, such as leaves, and remove them. Pour a bucketful of hot water down the drain to loosen the grease and debris. After this, pour 500g of soda crystals down the drain, then another bucketful of hot water to activate the crystals. Leave the crystals to work for 1 hour, then pour a third bucketful of hot water down the drain to flush out the soda crystals and any remaining debris. This is important as you don't want the soda crystals sitting in your drain and going hard. Repeat as necessary. For severe blockages, use a plunger or drain snake.

Car interiors and windscreens

Cleaning dashboards and other hard-surface interiors
WHITE VINEGAR

A 50/50 mix of white vinegar and water in a spray bottle is a
versatile and effective cleaner for most hard surfaces inside cars.
We recommend you spray it directly on to a cloth to clean, as this
will avoid accidental sprays on to the paintwork; then rub with
a clean cloth. If the solution does stray onto the paintwork,
rinse the area with water immediately and wipe dry.

Sparkling windscreens, inside and out
WHITE VINEGAR

Clean your windscreen inside and out with vinegar (50/50 mix with
water), but don't use it on windows when it's sunny as it'll evaporate
quickly and leave streaks. Avoid using it on tinted windows altogether,
because it may affect the adhesive tinted screen over time. To avoid
the paintwork, spray directly on to a dry cloth and buff the surface.
If you accidentally spray vinegar on to the paintwork, rinse the
area with water immediately and wipe dry.

Refreshing upholstery and carpets
WHITE VINEGAR

Spray a 50/50 mix of white vinegar and water lightly on to fabrics,
then rub with a dry cloth or sponge. For stubborn stains, allow
the vinegar/water to sit for 10 minutes before wiping. Beware of
using vinegar on leather furniture, as it may dry it out or damage
it over time.

INSECTS AND INVADERS

For the same reasons that we decided to stop using cleaning products full of toxic ingredients, we also wanted to be more mindful of the sprays, powders and bombs we deployed to deter insects and spiders from invading our homes. But what to do in the face of ant infestations, moths munching our clothes, flies crawling over our kitchen worktops and other unwelcome invaders? We didn't necessarily want to kill them all, we just wanted them to go elsewhere.

In the old days we were nukers. Purdy was an ace at fly-swatting and even now we both keep a fly swatter handy in a drawer. But we have learnt to take a more selective approach to bug battles, going for judicious deterrence rather than wholesale slaughter – not just because of the harsh chemicals involved in the latter, but also because we understand more about the delicate balance in nature maintained through the system of predation in the food chain.

Certain species of fly are important pollinators [xxiv] after all, and while some people are terrified of common house spiders, these useful creatures love to feast on flies and silverfish. Ladybirds eat aphids and microscopic parasitic wasps help control moths.

Welcome biodiversity in

According to Rob Dunn, whose book, *Never Home Alone*, is a fascinating deep delve into the evolution of our home environment, we share our homes with more than 200,000 different species of creature. Dunn is an American biologist who has spent years researching exactly who and what we live with, and how our daily environment affects us. From large insects and small arthropods to invisible bacteria and microscopically tiny viruses, the air we breathe contains a swarming mass of 'mostly benign life', and the more there is, the healthier we are likely to be. Many of these invisible beings benefit our immune systems. Dunn's message is clear, and it's a powerful one. Yes, of course, hygiene in certain places is essential. But we should all open our doors, welcome biodiversity in, put the harsh chemical sprays away and leave the spiders be.

Taking this on board, here are some natural remedies that will help keep insects off your countertops and moths off your woollies without harming your home biome.

- **Remove food sources** by regularly cleaning countertops and bins and vacuuming rugs and carpets. Keep open packets of dry food such as rice and flour sealed in containers like Kilner glass jars.

- **Before you put your winter woollies away**, ensure that they are laundered. This eradicates the keratin found in human skin, hair and nail clippings, as well as the food stains that moths love to feast on. Winter woollies should ideally be stored in sealed plastic bags in cupboards and drawers that have been deep cleaned using a spray bottle with neat rubbing alcohol or your multi-surface spray (see page 56).

- **Interrupt the breeding cycles of moths** by placing pheromone moth traps in the places they like to gather, such as behind furniture and bookcases and in the bottom of wardrobes.

- **Invest in cedarwood balls**, or use cotton wool balls and sprinkle them with a few drops of cedarwood oil. Place the balls in drawers, cupboards and the bags used to store your woollies, and refresh with the oil drops once a month.

- **Stop ant invasions** by sprinkling a line of bicarb where they are entering, or draw a line of chalk, or paint a line of liquid Castile soap with a paintbrush. They will try to find another route in, so stay vigilant.

~~~~~~~~~~

Our non-toxic insect deterrent spray for use on hard surfaces

For a good temporary deterrent for most insects (lasts for up to 1 hour), which can be sprayed on hard surfaces including windows,* make a solution of 50/50 vinegar and rubbing alcohol in a 300ml spray bottle and add 15 drops of citronella java essential oil and 15 drops of geranium essential oil. This is great in the summer when flies will be zooming in and out of open doors and windows. Be sure to label the bottle as it contains alcohol.

Avoid using anything containing vinegar on softer surfaces, such as marble or other natural stone or delicate, painted surfaces.

Bug spray for houseplants

Plants in sunny, dry conditions indoors are particularly prone to aphids or spider-mite infestation, but using this spray regularly will keep them healthy and bug free.

Mix ½ teaspoon of liquid Castile soap with 300ml of water in a spray bottle, and spritz the leaves. The spray won't harm the plants, but if you see an unsightly residue after a few days, follow up with a spray of just water.

SHELF LIFE: 2 WEEKS

Did you Know...

Mango farmers in Northern Australia have discovered they can boost their fruit crops by leaving out barrels of fish and animal carcasses. This attracts blowflies, which come and lay their eggs in the dead matter before foraging among flowers for nectar and protein-rich pollen, thus transporting pollen from one flower to another in the process. [xxv]

CHAPTER THREE

The Stain Bible

Throughout those years of discovery, beavering away in Purdy's garage, playing around with different combinations of natural minerals and plant-based, biodegradable soaps, we developed a proper passion for stain-busting. Our faces lit up each time someone brought in a new 'impossible-to-shift' stain and we'd set to work, determined to find the best combination of natural products and techniques to remove it. Our success rate was remarkable, and right from the start we both wanted to write a Stain Bible with simple instructions for tackling the most common stains on a multitude of fabrics and surfaces. All the solutions over the following pages use the hero ingredients you already have, so you will be able to reduce the number of bottles and stain removers you buy.

Clever stain removal is simply about being armed with the knowledge and the right natural products. Our objective is that by the end of this chapter, you will be able to restore a car-boot purchase to its former glory, rescue a 'ruined' white shirt from the bin and bring stained tablecloths back from the 'dust sheet' pile. You could even save yourself the financial and environmental cost of having to buy a new carpet. Above all, we hope that you'll never have to fork out for a shop-bought stain remover again – because, despite the mind-boggling number of options on the market, they don't always do the job they promise to.

There's quite a bit of conflicting information out there, too. Let's say you splash curry sauce on to your shirt or spill red wine over your friend's cream carpet. Most people panic and either start madly rubbing at the sauce with water or slosh a glass of white wine over the red, thinking it'll do the trick (it does sometimes: see page 131). Perhaps you're someone who stuffs a stained shirt into the laundry basket in the hope that the dried-on marks will miraculously vanish in the wash. If so, stop right there. You'll soon learn that a hot wash and hot air can actually bake stains in, sometimes for ever. Through years of trial and error (mostly trial — actually, a lot of trial), we have created natural stain-removal recipes that are bulletproof. Some are, frankly, miraculous, and we can't wait for you to try them out.

First things first: know your stain

If you're an impetuous type, you will doubtless want to skip this and turn straight to the stain-removal kit (see page 100), which provides specific solutions for just about every kind of stain we can think of, from avocado to vomit and beyond. But we urge you to bear with us. Because the first rule of stain removal is understanding what *type* of stain you are dealing with: protein, tannin, grease and oil, or a combination. We have also included what we've called outlier and mystery stains, which are none of the above and they too need special treatment. Understand the basic principles on this, and you will be armed for ever, even for the most unlikely stain situations.

Protein stains – any substance of human or animal origin. This includes urine, vomit, blood, poo, sweat, milk and eggs. Also, anything that *contains* proteins, such as grass and mud.

Oil and grease stains – self-explanatory and includes cooking oils, salad dressings, melted butter and pesto sauce.

Tannin stains – plant-derived stains, such as red wine, soy sauce, spinach, black tea or coffee, berries, beer, fruit and fruit juices.

Combination stains – stains containing several different staining compounds, such as protein and tannin. The most common are curry, bolognese, tomato sauce, chocolate, white coffee and tea, and make-up.

Outlier stains – one-offs that don't fit into the categories above, such as rust or scorch marks.

Mystery stains – when you have absolutely no idea what it is, or how it got there.

Try a long, cool soak

Having decided what type of stain you think you're dealing with, always start by scraping off any debris and soaking the fabric in cool water – ideally for anything from 2 to 24 hours – with an occasional agitation by hand. Soaking in cool water and then laundering is sometimes all you need for the stain to come right out. It sounds ridiculously simple, but 40% of fresh stains can be removed like this. Dried stains especially will benefit from a long, cool soak. However, if time is short, a cool rinse under a running tap is a good start.

Patience, patience, patience

According to The Smithsonian Museum Conservation Institute,[xxvi] which (among its other work) records cleaning practices through the ages, stain removal is 'sequential and repetitive'. The authors of an article entitled *Stain Removal* suggest that, for the toughest stains, you need to repeat stain-removal methods up to seven times. We have done this with Charlotte's turmeric-stained tablecloth with great results. In other words, dogged persistence works. Leave the stain removers time to get to work on your clothes and be prepared to keep going. If you can see you are removing a fraction of the stain each time you work on it, it should go completely (or nearly completely). Try turning your item inside out and work from the reverse of the fabric to the front, pushing the stain out and on to an old white towel or cloth. You can also help it from spreading by working from the edges towards the centre.

The return of the heroes

Of the seven heroes that you got to know in Chapter 2, five are as indispensable for stain removal as they are for cleaning. When you start using our stain-removal kit (see page 100), you will see that we give specific instructions for different stains using a combination of heroes, but here's our basic guide:

1. OXYGEN BLEACH [OB]

This is the most brilliant of all our stain shifters for most fabrics – *except wool, cashmere and silk.* It should be diluted in water and used either as a liquid solution or (for stubborn stains) applied as a granular paste. Remember: once diluted, oxygen bleach is active for only 6 hours.

Dissolve 1 tablespoon in 1 litre of hot water for light stains and 2 tablespoons per 1 litre for tougher ones, then leave the solution to cool. Let the clothes sit in the solution for 30 minutes, agitating gently every so often, then launder. Also, why not throw in some tea towels, sponges and cloths for a deep clean at the same time?

For really stubborn stains, sprinkle a few granules on to the stain, rub in with a little water and leave to sit for 15 minutes before putting the clothes in the solution to soak for 6 hours, then launder.

2. BICARB [BI]

Use bicarb as a paste to gently lift fresh stains from fabrics, particularly grease and protein stains. Make a thick paste with a little water, smear it on the stain and leave it for up to 1 hour, then launder. As a powder, it absorbs liquids and neutralises odours. Just sprinkle it on, leave it for a few minutes, then brush it away.

3. WHITE VINEGAR [WV]

A 50/50 mix of white vinegar and water is great at cutting through grease and oil stains. Spray it directly on to a fresh stain and agitate the fabric with your hands or a brush directly before laundering. Don't use it on delicate fabrics or protein stains as the acidity could set the stain.

4. RUBBING ALCOHOL [RA]

A great spot remover, rubbing alcohol is especially effective on grease and fresh ink stains, as it won't leave a watermark. Blot rather than rub the stain to remove any excess, then spray or pour rubbing alcohol on to a clean white paper towel or cloth and dab, if possible from the back.

5. SODA CRYSTALS [SC]

Diluted, soda crystals make an excellent pre-soak solution for oil and grease stains on most fabrics apart from silk, wool or cashmere. Dissolve 5 tablespoons of soda crystals in 500ml of hot water.

THE CHANGING OF THE COLOURS

Oxygen bleach will temporarily change the colour of many stains, but don't worry, this shows it is working. For example, powdered turmeric turns a raspberry colour; red wine turns dark grey/purple-blue (and interestingly, cheaper, cooking wine turns a tan colour); blood turns pinky-red; French mustard turns yellow and sometimes red; black tea turns light brown; grass turns acid green; and strawberries turn a rust colour.

Calling in the reinforcements

Alongside the five heroes we've already mentioned, there are several other pieces of kit that will simplify your stain removal, and we think are well worth the investment.

GALL SOAP

Used for hundreds of years as a miracle stain remover, gall soap contains ox-bile enzymes that make it effective on most stains, especially oil and protein stains. However, don't use it on tannin stains as this will seal them. It comes in liquid and solid-bar form (which can be netted, see below) and its great merit is that you can use it on silk, wool and cashmere. It has mild bleaching properties, so always test it on a hidden area.

NETTED STAIN BAR

This is a soap bar wrapped in some netting to provide an effective abrasive action. Our go-to soap bar for this is Marseille soap, another centuries-old wonder, which is traditionally made from natural plant oils with a high olive-oil content, and works well on most stains apart from tannin stains. You simply need to wrap it tightly in some plastic netting and secure it with a food-bag clip (the netting rescued from the little bags that your onions, garlic, oranges or lemons come in is ideal for this). For silk, wool and cashmere and delicate baby clothes, as well as upholstery and carpets, use the bar on its own. The method is the same whether you are using your bar netted or plain – just wet the soap, rub it on to the stain to work up a lather, and leave for 5 minutes; then rinse thoroughly and launder. For other eco stain bars, see page 167.

BABY SHAMPOO

Designed to clean body oils on delicate skin, this is ideal to gently remove stains from delicate fabrics such as wool, cashmere and silk. Rinse thoroughly in warm water – you don't want baby shampoo sluicing through your washing machine because the foam can damage it – and launder.

ECO LIQUID LAUNDRY DETERGENT

This is especially effective for embedded protein, ink and dye stains. Apply a small amount directly on to the stain and gently rub it into the fabric with a horsehair brush. Leave it to sit for 5 minutes, then rinse and launder.

SOAP VS DETERGENT: WHEN TO USE WHICH ONE AND WHAT'S THE DIFFERENCE BETWEEN THEM?

Soaps are made from natural ingredients – plant oils, vegetable fats and animal fats – reacted with lye (a strong alkali) in a process called saponification. We tend to think of soaps as more environmentally friendly than detergents, because the latter are often made from synthetic ingredients – usually of petrochemical origin. While soaps tend to have limited uses and can leave a scum residue, especially in hard-water areas, detergents – from the mildest baby shampoos to laundry liquids – are more versatile in terms of their use. It's a bit of a minefield, but all you need to remember is that, while you can use a detergent on any stain, you have to be careful with soap.

ECO WASHING-UP LIQUID

Slightly more heavy duty for greasy stains or make-up, washing-up liquid has been designed to break down fats and oils. Most commercial washing-up liquids are effective, but they can be harsh on fabrics. We prefer the eco versions. Apply a few drops directly to the stain, gently rub them into the fabric with a horsehair brush or between your hands and leave for 5 minutes. Rinse thoroughly in warm water (as with shampoo, you don't want washing-up liquid sluicing through your washing machine because the foam can damage it) and launder.

DISTILLED WATER

Distilled water in a spray bottle helps avoid the common problem of overwetting and leaving watermarks (caused by the impurities in tap water) on carpets and upholstery, so keep a bottle handy under your kitchen sink to use on any stain that can't be put through a washing machine. Dampen carpets and upholstery without getting them over-wet; then blot with a clean cloth or use a hairdryer on a low setting to help dry the area.

SOFT HORSEHAIR LAUNDRY BRUSH

This is a wonderfully useful piece of kit because it is gentle enough to scrub soap into a stain quite vigorously without the risk of damaging the fabric.

OLD WHITE TOWELS OR SHEETS

Cut into cloths, these can be used as pads beneath stains while you're working on them.

WHAT IF I DON'T HAVE...?

• If you don't have a horsehair brush, use a soft nail brush or the tips of your fingers in a circular motion.

• If you don't have eco liquid laundry detergent, use washing-up liquid as a stain pre-treatment, but rinse well before laundering.

• If you don't have a stain bar, try liquid hand soap or a bar of household soap, but avoid coloured soap.

• If you don't have rubbing alcohol, use vodka.

• If you don't have white vinegar, try wine vinegar.

RULES OF THE ROAD

Before you undertake any stain remedy, please read our rules of the road.

• **Never use oxygen bleach or soda crystals on silk, wool or cashmere**, as they will ruin the protein fibres.

• **Never put protein stains in hot water**, either to soak or to wash, as hot water will 'cook' the stain making it more difficult to remove.

• **Never use bar or liquid soaps on tannin stains**, as this will seal them.

• **Treat the stain as soon as possible**, ideally when still wet, as this will make the removal process far easier.

• **Never rub at a fresh stain**, as you will push it further into the fabric.

• **Work on stain from the reverse of the fabric if possible.**

• **Don't forget the power of a long, cool soak (ideally overnight)** – sometimes this is all you need before laundering.

- **Don't tumble dry and iron** as the heat may set your stain further. After working on the stain, leave it to air dry (residual stains may show only when the garment is dry) and tumble dry or iron only once you are sure the stain is out.

- **Don't ignore the care label** but do be aware that sometimes your stain won't come out at 30°C, and you will have to increase the temperature to what you think the fabric will withstand. Just use your judgement on this.

- **If you don't have the heroes to hand, it's always worth pre-treating any stain with a little liquid laundry detergent.** Rub it in with your fingers or a soft brush, leave for 5 minutes and launder.

- **Always test a hidden area first** – even for the products and solutions we recommend.

- **Don't give up.** If you see the stain going, persevere.

YOUR NATURAL STAIN-REMOVAL KIT

Here it is, the product of years of trial and error, and a great deal of blood, sweat and tears.

Silk, wool, cashmere, upholstery and carpets need a special approach, which we address on pages 129–35.

Treat each stain step by step, and move on to the next step only if you need to.

Always follow the Rules of the Road (see page 98).

~~~~~~

LEVEL OF DIFFICULTY

To help you assess what you are up against with any given stain, we have included a difficulty rating for each one.

 = Easy   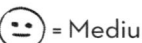 = Medium   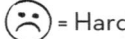 = Hard

AVOCADO (COMBINATION STAIN) ☺

Fresh Stain

1. Apply liquid laundry detergent with a brush or your fingers, leave for 15 minutes, launder. (An overnight soak and laundering also work, if you have the time and space.)
2. Use a netted stain bar (see page 94), leave for 15 minutes, launder.

Dry Stain

1. Cool water soak: 2+ hours. Apply liquid laundry detergent with a brush or your fingers, leave for 15 minutes, launder.
2. Use a netted stain bar (page 94), leave for 15 minutes, launder.
3. Soak in cooled oxygen-bleach solution (2 tablespoons OB to 1 litre warm water) for 6 hours, launder.

BAKED BEANS (COMBINATION STAIN) ☺

Fresh Stain

1. Cool water rinse, launder.
2. Apply liquid laundry detergent with a brush or fingers, leave for 15 minutes, launder.
3. Use a netted stain bar (page 94), launder.

Dry Stain

1. Cool water soak for 20+ minutes.
2. Apply liquid laundry detergent with a brush or your fingers, leave for 5 minutes, launder. (An overnight soak and laundering also work, if you have the time and space.)

- Never use oxygen bleach or soda crystals on silk, wool or cashmere.
- Treat each stain step by step, and move on to the next step only if you need to.
- Always follow the rules of the road (see page 98).

BALSAMIC VINEGAR AND OLIVE OIL

(COMBINATION STAIN)

Fresh Stain

1. Warm water rinse. Apply liquid laundry detergent using a brush or your fingers, leave for 5 minutes, launder. (An overnight soak and laundering also work, if you have the time and space.)

Dry Stain

1. Apply liquid laundry detergent using a brush or your fingers, leave for 15 minutes, launder.
2. Apply liquid soda crystals (test for colour fastness), launder immediately. If you don't have liquid soda crystals, use granules to make a soda-crystal solution (5 tablespoons SC in 500ml hot water) and soak for 2+ hours, then launder.

BARBECUE SAUCE (COMBINATION STAIN)

Fresh Stain

1. Warm water rinse. Apply liquid laundry detergent with a brush or your fingers, leave for 5 minutes, launder. (An overnight soak and laundering also work, if you have the time and space.)

Dry Stain

1. Apply liquid laundry detergent with a brush or your fingers, leave for 5 minutes, launder. (An overnight soak and laundering also work, if you have the time and space.)
2. Soak in cooled oxygen-bleach solution (2 tablespoons OB to 1 litre warm water) for 6 hours, launder.

- Never use oxygen bleach or soda crystals on silk, wool or cashmere.
- Treat each stain step by step, and move on to the next step only if you need to.
- Always follow the rules of the road (see page 98).

BEETROOT (TANNIN STAIN)

Fresh Stain

1. Warm water rinse, launder.
2. Apply liquid laundry detergent using a brush or your fingers, leave for 5 minutes, launder.
3. Soak in cooled oxygen-bleach solution (2 tablespoons OB to 1 litre warm water) for 2 hours, launder.

Dry Stain

1. Cool water soak for 30 minutes, launder.
2. Apply liquid laundry detergent using a brush or your fingers, leave for 5 minutes, launder.
3. Soak in cooled oxygen-bleach solution (2 tablespoons OB to 1 litre warm water) for 6 hours, launder.

BERRIES (TANNIN STAIN)

Fresh Stain

1. Warm water rinse, soak for 2 hours, launder.
2. Apply liquid laundry detergent with a brush or your fingers, leave for 5 minutes, launder.
3. Soak in cooled oxygen-bleach solution (2 tablespoons OB to 1 litre warm water) for 2 hours, launder.

Dry Stain

1. Warm water soak for 2+ hours. Apply liquid laundry detergent with a brush or your fingers, leave for 5 minutes, launder.
2. Soak in cooled oxygen-bleach solution (2 tablespoons OB to 1 litre warm water) for 4 hours, launder.

- Never use oxygen bleach or soda crystals on silk, wool or cashmere.
- Treat each stain step by step, and move on to the next step only if you need to.
- Always follow the rules of the road (see page 98).

BLOOD (PROTEIN STAIN)

Fresh Stain
1. Cool water soak for 2+ hours, launder.
2. Soak in cooled oxygen-bleach solution (2 tablespoons OB to 1 litre warm water) for 2 hours, launder.

Dry Stain
1. Cool water soak for 6+ hours, launder.
2. Soak in cooled oxygen-bleach solution (2 tablespoons OB to 1 litre warm water) for 6 hours, launder.

BOLOGNESE (COMBINATION STAIN)

Fresh Stain
1. Cool water rinse. Apply liquid laundry detergent with a brush or your fingers, leave for 5 minutes, launder.
2. Use a netted stain bar (page 94), launder.
3. Soak in cooled oxygen bleach solution (2 tbsp OB to 1 litre warm water) for 4 hours, launder.

Dry Stain
1. Cool water soak for 1+ hour. Apply liquid laundry detergent with a brush or your fingers, leave for 5 minutes, launder.
2. Use a netted stain bar (page 94), launder.
3. Soak in cooled oxygen-bleach solution (2 tablespoons OB to 1 litre warm water) for 6 hours, launder.

- Never use oxygen bleach or soda crystals on silk, wool or cashmere.
- Treat each stain step by step, and move on to the next step only if you need to.
- Always follow the rules of the road (see page 98).

CALPOL (OUTLIER STAIN) ☺

Fresh Stain

1. Cool water rinse. Apply liquid laundry detergent with a brush or fingers, leave for 5 minutes, launder.
2. Use a netted stain bar (page 94), cool water rinse, launder.

Dry Stain

1. Cool water soak 1+ hour. Apply liquid laundry detergent with a brush or your fingers, leave for 5 minutes, launder.
2. Use a netted stain bar (page 94), cool water rinse, launder.

CANDLE WAX (OIL AND GREASE STAIN) ☺

Fresh Stain

1. Freeze until brittle: 6+ hours. Scrape off any excess when still brittle, put a brown paper on top of the wax and pass a hot iron over the paper to absorb the remaining wax.
2. Soak in cooled soda-crystal solution (5 tablespoons SC in 500ml hot water) for 6 hours, cool water rinse. Rub in liquid laundry detergent with a brush or your fingers, leave for 10 minutes, launder.
3. If the candle colour is still visible, soak in cooled oxygen-bleach solution (2 tablespoons OB to 1 litre warm water) for 6 hours, launder.

Dry Stain *As for fresh*

- Never use oxygen bleach or soda crystals on silk, wool or cashmere.
- Treat each stain step by step, and move on to the next step only if you need to.
- Always follow the rules of the road (see page 98).

CARROTS (TANNIN STAIN) ☺

Fresh Stain

1. Apply liquid laundry detergent using a brush or fingers, leave for 5 minutes, launder. (An overnight soak and laundering also work, if you have the time and space.)
2. Soak in cooled oxygen-bleach solution (2 tablespoons OB to 1 litre warm water) for 2 hours, launder.

Dry Stain

1. Apply liquid laundry detergent using a brush or your fingers , leave for 5 minutes, launder. (An overnight soak and laundering also work, if you have the time and space.)
2. Soak in cooled oxygen-bleach solution (2 tablespoons OB to 1 litre warm water) for 6 hours, launder.

CHEWING GUM (OIL AND GREASE STAIN) 😐

Fresh Stain

1. Freeze until really brittle: 6+ hours. Scrape off any excess with a knife, dab with rubbing alcohol or a 50/50 mix of white vinegar and water, rinse in warm water. Apply liquid laundry detergent with a brush or your fingers, leave for 5 minutes, launder.

Dry Stain *As for fresh*

- Never use oxygen bleach or soda crystals on silk, wool or cashmere.
- Treat each stain step by step, and move on to the next step only if you need to.
- Always follow the rules of the road (see page 98).

CHILLI SAUCE (COMBINATION STAIN) 😖

Fresh Stain

1. Apply liquid laundry detergent with a brush or your fingers, leave for 5 minutes, launder.
2. Use a netted stain bar (page 94), launder.
3. Soak in cooled oxygen bleach solution (2 tablespoons OB to 1 litre warm water) for 2 hours, launder.

Dry Stain

1. Cool water soak for 6+ hours. Apply liquid laundry detergent with a brush or your fingers, leave for 5 minutes, launder.
2. Use a netted stain bar (page 94), launder.
3. Soak in cooled oxygen-bleach solution (2 tablespoons OB to 1 litre warm water) for 6 hours, launder.

CHOCOLATE (COMBINATION STAIN) 😕

For chocolate on carpets and upholstery see page 134.

Fresh Stain

1. Cool water soak for 5 minutes. Apply liquid laundry detergent using a brush or your fingers, leave for 5 minutes, launder.
2. Soak in cooled oxygen bleach solution (2 tablespoons OB to 1 litre warm water) for 30 minutes, launder.

Dry Stain

1. Cool water soak for 2 hours. Apply liquid laundry detergent using a brush or your fingers, leave for 5 minutes, launder.
2. Soak in cooled oxygen-bleach solution (2 tablespoons OB to 1 litre warm water) for 2 hours, launder.

- Never use oxygen bleach or soda crystals on silk, wool or cashmere.
- Treat each stain step by step, and move on to the next step only if you need to.
- Always follow the rules of the road (see page 98).

COCA-COLA (TANNIN STAIN) ☺

Fresh Stain

1. Warm water rinse, launder.
2. Apply liquid laundry detergent using a brush or your fingers, leave for 5 minutes, launder. (An overnight soak and laundering also work, if you have the time and space.)

Dry Stain

1. Warm water soak for 2 hours. Apply liquid laundry detergent using a brush or your fingers, leave for 5 minutes, launder. (An overnight soak and laundering also work, if you have the time and space.)
2. Soak in cooled oxygen-bleach solution (2 tablespoons OB to 1 litre warm water) for 6 hours, launder.

COFFEE, BLACK (TANNIN STAIN) ☺

Fresh Stain

1. Warm water rinse. Apply liquid laundry detergent using a brush or your fingers, leave for 5 minutes, launder. (An overnight soak and laundering also work, if you have the time and space.)

Dry Stain

1. Apply liquid laundry detergent using a brush or your fingers, leave for 5 minutes, launder. (An overnight soak and laundering also work, if you have the time and space).
2. Soak in cooled oxygen-bleach solution (2 tablespoons OB to 1 litre warm water) for 6 hours, launder.

- Never use oxygen bleach or soda crystals on silk, wool or cashmere.
- Treat each stain step by step, and move on to the next step only if you need to.
- Always follow the rules of the road (see page 98).

COFFEE, WHITE (COMBINATION STAIN) 😐

Fresh Stain

1. Warm water rinse, launder.
2. Apply liquid laundry detergent with a brush or your fingers, leave for 5 minutes, launder. (An overnight soak and laundering also work, if you have the time and space.)

Dry Stain

1. Apply liquid laundry detergent with a brush or your fingers, leave for 5 minutes, launder. (An overnight soak and laundering also work, if you have the time and space.)
2. Use a netted stain bar (page 94), launder.
3. Soak in cooled oxygen-bleach solution (2 tablespoons OB to 1 litre warm water) for 1 hour, launder.

COLLAR, DIRT RING (PROTEIN STAIN) ☹

Fresh Stain

1. Cool water rinse, use netted gall soap (page 94), leave for 10 minutes, launder.
2. Apply liquid laundry detergent, rubbing in a pinch of oxygen bleach granules with a brush or your fingers, leave for 10 minutes, launder.
3. Soak in cooled oxygen-bleach solution (2 tablespoons OB to 1 litre warm water) for 6 hours, launder.

Dry Stain

1. Cool water soak for 4+ hours. Use netted gall soap (see page 94), cool water rinse, launder.
2. Apply liquid laundry detergent, rubbing in a pinch of oxygen-bleach granules with a brush or your fingers, leave for 30 minutes, launder.
3. Soak in cooled oxygen-bleach solution (2 tablespoons OB to 1 litre warm water) for 6 hours, launder.

- Never use oxygen bleach or soda crystals on silk, wool or cashmere.
- Treat each stain step by step, and move on to the next step only if you need to.
- Always follow the rules of the road (see page 98).

CRANBERRY SAUCE (TANNIN STAIN)

Fresh Stain

1. Warm water rinse, apply liquid laundry detergent with a brush or your fingers, leave for 5 minutes, launder.

Dry Stain

1. Warm water rinse, apply liquid laundry detergent, rubbing in a pinch of oxygen-bleach granules with a brush or your fingers, leave for 5 minutes, launder.
2. Soak in cooled oxygen-bleach solution (2 tablespoons OB to 1 litre warm water) for 6 hours, launder.

CREAM (OIL AND GREASE STAIN)

Fresh Stain

1. Warm water rinse, launder. (An overnight soak and laundering also work, if you have the time and space.)
2. Apply liquid laundry detergent with a brush or your fingers, leave for 5 minutes, launder.

Dry Stain

1. Warm water soak for 1 hour. Apply liquid laundry detergent with a brush or your fingers, leave for 5 minutes, launder.
2. Soak in soda-crystal solution (5 tablespoons SC in 500ml hot water) for 2+ hours , launder.

- Never use oxygen bleach or soda crystals on silk, wool or cashmere.
- Treat each stain step by step, and move on to the next step only if you need to.
- Always follow the rules of the road (see page 98).

CREAM CHEESE (OIL AND GREASE STAIN) ☺

Fresh Stain

1. Warm water soak for 10 minutes. Apply liquid laundry detergent with a brush or your fingers, leave for 5 minutes, launder.

Dry Stain

1. Warm water soak for 2+ hours. Apply liquid laundry detergent with a brush or your fingers, leave for 5 minutes, launder.

CURRY (COMBINATION STAIN) ☹

This is absolutely, without doubt one of the most difficult stains to remove when dry, so it is worth dealing with it as soon as you can and, at the very least, keeping it damp. If you have let the stain dry, repeated soaking in oxygen bleach and using netted gall soap will eventually produce results.

Fresh Stain

1. Cool water rinse, soak in cooled oxygen-bleach solution (2 tablespoons OB to 1 litre warm water) for 2+ hours, launder.
2. Use netted gall soap (page 94), launder.
3. Soak in cooled oxygen-bleach solution (2 tablespoons OB to 1 litre warm water) for 4 hours, launder.

Dry Stain

1. Cool water soak 1+ hour (overnight if possible).
2. Use netted gall soap (page 94), leave for 15 minutes, launder.
3. Soak in cooled oxygen-bleach solution (2 tablespoons OB to 1 litre warm water) for 6 hours, launder.
4. Repeat steps 2 and 3 until the stain is very faint or gone.

- Never use oxygen bleach or soda crystals on silk, wool or cashmere.
- Treat each stain step by step, and move on to the next step only if you need to.
- Always follow the rules of the road (see page 98).

EGG (PROTEIN STAIN / EASY) ☺

Fresh Stain

1. Cool water rinse, apply liquid laundry detergent with a brush or your fingers, leave for 5 minutes, launder. (An overnight soak and laundering also work, if you have the time and space.)

Dry Stain

1. Cool water soak: 2+ hours. Apply liquid laundry detergent with a brush or your fingers, leave for 5 minutes, launder.
2. Use a netted stain bar or netted gall soap (page 94), leave for 5 minutes, launder.
3. Soak in cooled oxygen-bleach solution (2 tablespoons OB to 1 litre warm water) for 6 hours, launder.

FAECES (PROTEIN STAIN) ☺

Fresh Stain

1. Cool water rinse through back of the fabric under running tap, cool water soak for 1 hour. Use a netted stain bar or netted gall soap (page 94), leave for 15 minutes, launder.
2. Soak in cooled oxygen-bleach solution (2 tablespoons OB to 1 litre warm water) for 2 hours, launder.

Dry Stain

1. Cool water rinse through fabric reverse under running tap, cool water soak for 6+ hours. Use a netted stain bar or netted gall soap (page 94), leave for 30 minutes, launder.
2. Soak in cooled oxygen-bleach solution (2 tablespoons OB to 1 litre warm water) for 6 hours, launder.

- Never use oxygen bleach or soda crystals on silk, wool or cashmere.
- Treat each stain step by step, and move on to the next step only if you need to.
- Always follow the rules of the road (see page 98).

FRUIT JUICE (TANNIN STAIN) ☺

Fresh Stain

1. Warm water rinse under running tap, soak for 1+ hour. Apply liquid laundry detergent with a brush or your fingers, leave for 5 minutes, launder.
2. Soak in cooled oxygen-bleach solution (2 tablespoons OB to 1 litre warm water) for 1 hour, launder.

Dry Stain

1. Soak in cooled oxygen-bleach solution (2 tablespoons OB to 1 litre warm water) for 6 hours, launder.

GRASS (PROTEIN STAIN) ☹

Often a grass stain will be combined with mud and can be very stubborn. If so, leave the mud to dry and brush off the excess before treating.

Fresh Stain

1. Cool water soak for 2+ hours. Apply liquid laundry detergent with a brush or fingers, leave for 5 minutes, launder.
2. Soak in cooled oxygen-bleach solution (2 tablespoons OB to 1 litre warm water) for 6 hours, launder.
3. Use netted gall soap (page 94), leave for 15 minutes, launder.

Dry Stain *As for fresh*

- Never use oxygen bleach or soda crystals on silk, wool or cashmere.
- Treat each stain step by step, and move on to the next step only if you need to.
- Always follow the rules of the road (see page 98).

GRAVY (COMBINATION STAIN) 😊

Fresh Stain

1. Cool water rinse, apply liquid laundry detergent with a brush or your fingers, leave for 5 minutes, launder. (An overnight soak and laundering also work, if you have the time and space.)
2. Use a netted stain bar (page 94) and leave for 10 minutes, launder.

Dry Stain

1. Cool water soak for 1+ hour. Apply liquid laundry detergent with a brush or your fingers, leave for 5 minutes, launder. (An overnight soak and laundering also work, if you have the time and space.)
2. Use a netted stain bar (page 94), leave for 10 minutes, launder.
3. Soak in cooled oxygen-bleach solution (2 tablespoons OB to 1 litre warm water) 6 hours, launder.

ICE CREAM (COMBINATION STAIN) 😊

Fresh Stain

1. Warm water rinse, launder.
2. Apply liquid laundry detergent with a brush or your fingers, leave for 5 minutes, launder. (An overnight soak and laundering also work, if you have the time and space.)

Dry Stain

1. Apply liquid laundry detergent with a brush or your fingers, leave for 10 minutes, launder. (An overnight soak and laundering also work, if you have the time and space.)
2. Use a netted stain bar (page 94), leave for 10 minutes, launder.
3. Soak in cooled oxygen-bleach solution (2 tablespoons OB to 1 litre warm water) for 2 hours, launder.

- Never use oxygen bleach or soda crystals on silk, wool or cashmere.
- Treat each stain step by step, and move on to the next step only if you need to.
- Always follow the rules of the road (see page 98).

INK, GEL PEN, BIRO, HIGHLIGHTER
(OUTLIER STAIN)

Fresh Stain

1. Blot, then dab rubbing alcohol from the reverse of the fabric on to a clean white pad so you can see the colour coming out; cool water rinse. Apply liquid laundry detergent with a brush or your fingers, leave for 10 minutes, launder.
2. Use netted gall soap (page 94) , launder.
3. Soak in cooled soda-crystal solution (5 tablespoons SC in 500ml hot water) for 2 hours, cool water rinse, launder.

Dry Stain *As for fresh*

KETCHUP (COMBINATION STAIN)

Fresh Stain

1. Cool water rinse, apply liquid laundry detergent with a brush or your fingers, leave for 5 minutes, launder. (An overnight soak and laundering also work, if you have the time and space.)

Dry Stain

1. Cool water soak for 2+ hours, apply liquid laundry detergent with a brush or your fingers, leave for 5 minutes, launder. (An overnight soak and laundering also work, if you have the time and space.)
2. Use a netted stain bar (page 94), launder.

- Never use oxygen bleach or soda crystals on silk, wool or cashmere.
- Treat each stain step by step, and move on to the next step only if you need to.
- Always follow the rules of the road (see page 98).

LIPSTICK (OIL AND GREASE STAIN) ☺

Lipstick can be tricky.

Fresh Stain

1. Apply liquid laundry detergent using a brush or your fingers, leave for 5 minutes, launder.
2. Soak in soda-crystal solution (5 tablespoons SC in 500ml hot water) for 2 hours, launder.
3. Soak in oxygen-bleach solution (2 tablespoons OB to 1 litre warm water) for 6 hours, launder.

Dry Stain *As for fresh*

MAKE-UP (OIL AND GREASE STAIN) ☺

Fresh Stain

1. Warm water rinse, apply liquid laundry detergent with a brush or your fingers, leave for 5 minutes, launder.
2. Use a netted stain bar (page 94), launder.
3. Soak in soda-crystal solution (5 tablespoons SC in 500ml hot water) for 2 hours , launder.

Dry Stain

1. Warm water rinse, apply liquid laundry detergent with a brush or your fingers, leave for 5 minutes, launder.
2. Soak in soda-crystal solution (5 tablespoons SC in 500ml hot water) for 2 hours , launder.
3. Use a netted stain bar (page 94), launder.

- Never use oxygen bleach or soda crystals on silk, wool or cashmere.
- Treat each stain step by step, and move on to the next step only if you need to.
- Always follow the rules of the road (see page 98).

MASCARA (OIL AND GREASE STAIN) 😕

Fresh Stain

1. Apply liquid laundry detergent with a brush or your fingers, leave for 5 minutes, launder.
2. Soak in soda-crystal solution (5 tablespoons SC in 500ml hot water) for 6+ hours, launder.
3. Use a netted stain bar (page 94), leave for 10 minutes, launder.

Dry Stain

1. Apply liquid laundry detergent with a brush or your fingers, leave for 5 minutes, launder.
2. Use a netted stain bar (page 94), leave for 10 minutes, launder.
3. Soak in soda-crystal solution (7 tablespoons SC in 500ml hot water) for 6+ hours, launder.

MAYONNAISE (OIL AND GREASE STAIN) 🙂

Fresh Stain

1. Warm water rinse, apply liquid laundry detergent with a brush or your fingers, leave for 5 minutes, launder. (An overnight soak and laundering also work, if you have the time and space.)

Dry Stain

1. Warm water rinse, apply liquid laundry detergent with a brush or your fingers, leave for 5 minutes, launder.
2. Use a netted stain bar (page 94), leave for 10 minutes, launder.

- Never use oxygen bleach or soda crystals on silk, wool or cashmere.
- Treat each stain step by step, and move on to the next step only if you need to.
- Always follow the rules of the road (see page 98).

MILK (PROTEIN STAIN) 😊

Fresh Stain
1. Cool water rinse, apply liquid laundry detergent with a brush or your fingers, leave for 5 minutes, launder. (An overnight soak and laundering also work, if you have the time and space.)

Dry Stain
1. Cool water soak for 1+ hour, apply liquid laundry detergent with a brush or your fingers, leave for 5 minutes, launder. (An overnight soak and laundering also work, if you have the time and space.)
2. Use a netted stain bar (page 94), launder.

MUD (PROTEIN STAIN) 🙁

Mud stains can be very stubborn – it is worth being persistent.
Always allow them to dry first. (For mud on carpets, see page 133.)

Dry Stain
1. Scrape, brush or vacuum off any excess, cool water soak for 2+ hours, apply liquid laundry detergent using a brush or your fingers, leave for 15 minutes, launder.
2. Soak in cooled oxygen-bleach solution (2 tablespoons OB to 1 litre warm water) for 6 hours, launder.
3. Use netted gall soap (page 94), leave for 15 minutes, launder.

- Never use oxygen bleach or soda crystals on silk, wool or cashmere.
- Treat each stain step by step, and move on to the next step only if you need to.
- Always follow the rules of the road (see page 98).

MUSTARD (COMBINATION STAIN) ☺

Yellow mustard can be tricky because it often contains turmeric.

Fresh Stain

1. Cool water rinse, apply liquid laundry detergent with a brush or your fingers, leave for 5 minutes, launder. (An overnight soak and laundering also work, if you have the time and space.)
2. Use a netted stain bar (page 94), leave for 10 minutes, launder.
3. Soak in cooled oxygen-bleach solution (2 tablespoons OB to 1 litre warm water) for 1+ hour, launder.

Dry Stain

1. Cool water soak for 2+ hours, apply liquid laundry detergent with a brush or your fingers, leave for 5 minutes, launder.
2. Use a netted stain bar (page 94), leave for 10 minutes, launder.
3. Soak in cooled oxygen-bleach solution (2 tablespoons OB to 1 litre warm water) for 2+ hours, launder.

OIL AND GREASE SPLATTERS ☺

(OIL AND GREASE STAIN / EASY)

Fresh Stain

1. Warm water soak for 20 minutes, apply liquid laundry detergent with a brush or your fingers, leave for 15 minutes, launder. (An overnight soak and laundering also work, if you have the time and space.)

Dry Stain

1. Warm water soak for 1 hour, apply liquid laundry detergent with a brush or fingers, leave for 30 minutes, launder.
2. Soak in soda-crystal solution (5 tablespoons SC in 500ml hot water) overnight, launder.

- Never use oxygen bleach or soda crystals on silk, wool or cashmere.
- Treat each stain step by step, and move on to the next step only if you need to.
- Always follow the rules of the road (see page 98).

PAINT, OIL-BASED (COMBINATION STAIN)

Fresh Stain

1. Dab the reverse of the stain with a solvent such as white spirit on to a white cloth so you can see the colour coming out. Apply liquid laundry detergent with a brush or your fingers, leave for 15 minutes, launder.

Dry Stain *As for fresh*

PAINT, WATER-BASED (COMBINATION STAIN)

Fresh Stain

1. Warm water rinse, apply liquid laundry detergent with a brush or your fingers, leave for 5 minutes, launder.

Dry Stain

1. Warm water rinse, soak for 6+ hours, apply liquid laundry detergent with a brush or your fingers, leave for 30 minutes, launder.

PESTO (COMBINATION STAIN)

Fresh Stain

1. Warm water rinse, apply liquid laundry detergent with a brush or your fingers, leave for 5 minutes, launder.
2. Use a netted stain bar (page 94), launder.
3. Soak in soda-crystal solution (5 tablespoons SC in 500ml hot water) for 2+ hours, launder.

Dry Stain

1. Warm water rinse, apply liquid laundry detergent with a brush or your fingers, leave for 20 minutes, launder.
2. Use a netted stain bar (page 94), launder.
3. Soak in soda-crystal solution (5 tablespoons SC in 500ml hot water) for 6+ hours, launder.

- Never use oxygen bleach or soda crystals on silk, wool or cashmere.
- Treat each stain step by step, and move on to the next step only if you need to.
- Always follow the rules of the road (see page 98).

RUST (OUTLIER STAIN)

Fresh Stain *Treat as dry*

Dry Stain

1. Squeeze a generous amount of lemon juice on to the stain.
2. Leave in daylight 1+ hour, cool water rinse, launder.
3. Repeat.

SALAD DRESSING (COMBINATION STAIN)

Fresh Stain

1. Warm water rinse under running tap, apply liquid laundry detergent with a brush or your fingers, leave for 5 minutes, launder.
2. Use a netted stain bar (page 94), launder.

Dry Stain

1. Warm water soak for 20 minutes, apply liquid laundry detergent with a brush or your fingers, leave for 5 minutes, launder.
2. Use a netted stain bar (page 94), launder.
3. Soak in soda-crystal solution (5 tablespoons SC in 500ml hot water) for 6+ hours, launder.

SCORCH MARKS, LIGHT (OUTLIER STAIN)

Fresh Stain *Treat as dry*

Dry Stain

1. Cool water soak for 12 hours, agitating occasionally; launder.
2. Repeat cool water soak and launder, if necessary.
3. Lay the fabric in sunlight to dry.

- Never use oxygen bleach or soda crystals on silk, wool or cashmere.
- Treat each stain step by step, and move on to the next step only if you need to.
- Always follow the rules of the road (see page 98).

SHOE POLISH (OIL AND GREASE) ☹

Fresh Stain

1. Apply liquid laundry detergent with a brush or your fingers, leave for 5 minutes, launder.
2. Use a netted stain bar (page 94), leave for 5 minutes, launder.
3. Soak in oxygen-bleach solution (2 tablespoons OB to 1 litre warm water) for 4 hours, launder.

Dry Stain

1. Apply liquid laundry detergent with a brush or your fingers, leave for 30 minutes, launder.
2. Use a netted stain bar (page 94), leave for 30 minutes, launder.
3. Soak in oxygen-bleach solution (2 tablespoons OB to 1 litre warm water) for 6 hours, launder.

SOY SAUCE (TANNIN STAIN) ☺

Fresh Stain

1. Warm water rinse, launder. (An overnight soak and laundering also work, if you have the time and space.)
2. Apply liquid laundry detergent using a brush or your fingers, leave for 5 minutes, launder.

Dry Stain

1. Soak 1+ hour, apply liquid laundry detergent using a brush or your fingers, leave for 5 minutes, launder.
2. Soak in cooled oxygen bleach solution (2 tablespoons OB to 1 litre warm water) for 6 hours, launder.

- Never use oxygen bleach or soda crystals on silk, wool or cashmere.
- Treat each stain step by step, and move on to the next step only if you need to.
- Always follow the rules of the road (see page 98).

SPINACH (COMBINATION STAIN) 😐

Fresh Stain

1. Cool water rinse, apply liquid laundry detergent with a brush or your fingers, leave for 5 minutes, launder.
2. Use a netted stain bar (page 94), launder.

Dry Stain

1. Cool water soak 1+ hour, apply liquid laundry detergent with a brush or your fingers, leave for 5 minutes, launder.
2. Use a netted stain bar (page 94), launder.
3. Soak in cooled oxygen-bleach solution (2 tablespoons OB to 1 litre warm water) for 2 hours, launder.

SUNSCREEN (OIL AND GREASE STAIN) 😐

Fresh Stain

1. Warm water rinse, Apply liquid laundry detergent with a brush or your fingers, leave for 5 minutes, launder.
2. Use a netted stain bar (page 94), launder.
3. Soak in cooled oxygen-bleach solution (2 tablespoons OB to 1 litre warm water) for 2 hours, launder.

Dry Stain *As for fresh*

- Never use oxygen bleach or soda crystals on silk, wool or cashmere.
- Treat each stain step by step, and move on to the next step only if you need to.
- Always follow the rules of the road (see page 98).

SWEAT (PROTEIN STAIN) 😣

Sweat stains are difficult stain to get rid of and require persistence.

Fresh Stain

1. Spray with a 50/50 mix of white vinegar and water, leave for 15 minutes, cool water soak for 2+ hours, launder.
2. Use netted gall soap (page 94), leave for 15 minutes, launder.
3. Repeat netted gall soap, rubbing in a pinch of oxygen-bleach granules with a brush or your fingers, leave for 15 minutes, launder.
4. Soak in cooled oxygen-bleach solution (2 tablespoons OB to 1 litre warm water) for 6 hours, launder.

Dry Stain *As for fresh*

TEA, BLACK (TANNIN STAIN) 😊

Fresh Stain

1. Warm water rinse, launder.
2. Apply liquid laundry detergent using a brush or your fingers, leave for 5 minutes, launder. (An overnight soak and laundering also work, if you have the time and space.)
3. Soak in cooled oxygen-bleach solution (2 tablespoons OB to 1 litre warm water) for 1 hour, launder.

Dry Stain

1. Apply liquid laundry detergent using a brush or your fingers, leave for 5 minutes, launder. (An overnight soak and laundering also work, if you have the time and space.)
2. Soak in cooled oxygen-bleach solution (2 tablespoons OB to 1 litre warm water) for 1 hour, launder.

- Never use oxygen bleach or soda crystals on silk, wool or cashmere.
- Treat each stain step by step, and move on to the next step only if you need to.
- Always follow the rules of the road (see page 98).

TEA, WITH MILK (COMBINATION STAIN)

Fresh Stain

1. Warm water rinse, launder.
2. Apply liquid laundry detergent using a brush or your fingers, leave for 5 minutes, launder. (An overnight soak and laundering also work, if you have the time and space.)

Dry Stain

1. Warm water soak for 1+ hour, apply liquid laundry detergent using a brush or your fingers, leave for 5 minutes, launder. (An overnight soak and laundering also work, if you have the time and space.)
2. Soak in oxygen-bleach solution (2 tablespoons OB to 1 litre warm water) when cool for 6 hours, launder.

TOMATO PASTA SAUCE (COMBINATION STAIN) 😣

This can be a tricky stain and needs persistence.

Fresh Stain

1. Cool water rinse under running tap, apply liquid laundry detergent with a brush or your fingers, leave for 5 minutes, launder.
2. Use a netted stain bar (page 94) and leave to sit for 10 minutes, launder.
3. Soak in cooled oxygen-bleach solution (2 tablespoons OB to 1 litre warm water) for 2 hours, launder.

Dry Stain

1. Cool water soak for 6+ hours, apply liquid laundry detergent with a brush or your fingers, leave for 30+ minutes, launder.
2. Use a netted stain bar (page 94), leave for 10 minutes, launder.
3. Soak in cooled oxygen-bleach solution (2 tablespoons OB to 1 litre warm water) for 6 hours, launder.

- Never use oxygen bleach or soda crystals on silk, wool or cashmere.
- Treat each stain step by step, and move on to the next step only if you need to.
- Always follow the rules of the road (see page 98).

TOOTHPASTE (OUTLIER STAIN)

Fresh Stain
1. Cool water rinse, apply liquid laundry detergent with a brush or your fingers, leave for 5 minutes, launder.
2. Use a netted stain bar (page 94), launder.
3. Soak in cooled soda-crystal solution (5 tablespoons SC in 500ml hot water) for 2 hours, launder.

Dry Stain
1. Cool water rinse, apply liquid laundry detergent with a brush or your fingers, launder.
2. Use a netted stain bar (page 94), launder.
3. Soak in cooled soda-crystal solution (5 tablespoons SC in 500ml hot water) for 6 hours.

TURMERIC POWDER (COMBINATION STAIN)

Fresh Stain
1. Scrape or shake off any excess, cool water soak overnight, apply liquid laundry detergent with a brush or your fingers, leave for 10 minutes, launder.
2. Use a netted stain bar (page 94), leave for 10 minutes , launder.
3. Soak in cooled oxygen-bleach solution (2 tablespoons OB to 1 litre warm water) for 2 hours, launder.

Dry Stain *As for fresh*

- Never use oxygen bleach or soda crystals on silk, wool or cashmere.
- Treat each stain step by step, and move on to the next step only if you need to.
- Always follow the rules of the road (see page 98).

URINE (PROTEIN STAIN) 😕

For urine on carpets, see page 132-3.

Fresh Stain

1. Cool water rinse, use a netted stain bar (see page 94), leave for 10 minutes, launder.
2. Soak in cooled oxygen-bleach solution (2 tablespoons OB to 1 litre warm water) for 2 hours, launder.

Dry Stain

1. Cool water soak for 1 hour, use a netted stain bar (page 94), leave for 10 minutes, launder.
2. Soak in cooled oxygen-bleach solution (2 tablespoons OB to 1 litre warm water) for 6 hours, launder.

VOMIT (PROTEIN STAIN) 😕

For vomit on carpets, see page 133.

Fresh Stain

1. Cool water soak for 2 hours. Apply liquid laundry detergent with a brush or your fingers, leave for 5 minutes, launder.
2. Use a netted stain bar (page 94), leave for 10 minutes, launder.
3. Soak in cooled oxygen-bleach solution (2 tablespoons OB to 1 litre warm water) for 6 hours, launder.

Dry Stain

1. Cool water soak overnight, apply liquid laundry detergent with a brush or your fingers, leave for 10 minutes, launder.
2. Use a netted stain bar (page 94), leave for 10 minutes, launder.
3. Soak in cooled oxygen-bleach solution (2 tablespoons OB to 1 litre warm water) for 6 hours, launder.

- Never use oxygen bleach or soda crystals on silk, wool or cashmere.
- Treat each stain step by step, and move on to the next step only if you need to.
- Always follow the rules of the road (see page 98).

WINE, RED (TANNIN STAIN) 🙂

For red wine on carpets see pages 131–2.

Fresh Stain

1. Blot any excess with kitchen paper, overnight soak, launder.
2. Soak in cooled oxygen-bleach solution (2 tablespoons OB to 1 litre warm water) for 5 minutes, launder.

Dry Stain

1. Overnight soak, apply liquid laundry detergent with a brush or your fingers, leave for 5 mintues, launder.
2. Soak in cooled oxygen-bleach solution (2 tablespoons OB to 1 litre warm water) for 1 hour, launder.

MYSTERY STAINS 🙁

Fresh Stain

1. Cool water soak overnight, launder.
2. Apply liquid laundry detergent with a brush or your fingers, leave for 15 minutes, launder.
3. Use a netted stain bar (page 94), leave for 15 minutes, launder.
4. Soak in cooled oxygen-bleach solution (2 tablespoon OB to 1 litre warm water) for 1 hour, launder.

Dry Stain

1. Cool water soak overnight, apply liquid laundry detergent with a brush or your fingers, leave for 15 minutes, launder.
2. Use a netted stain bar (page 94), leave for 15 minutes, launder.
3. Soak in cooled oxygen-bleach solution (2 tablespoons OB to 1 litre warm water) for 6 hours, launder.

- Never use oxygen bleach or soda crystals on silk, wool or cashmere.
- Treat each stain step by step, and move on to the next step only if you need to.
- Always follow the rules of the road (see page 98).

SPECIAL CASES

While our stain-removal kit offers bulletproof remedies for getting most stains out of most fabrics, when it comes to silk, wool and cashmere, or wool, wool mix and synthetic carpets, the rules are a little different. The same is true for upholstery fabrics, for the obvious reason that they can't go in a washing machine.

Silk fabrics

For silk fabrics, wet the stained area with cool water then, depending on the stain (see page 90), gently rub in gall soap, baby shampoo or a mild eco detergent (we like to use baby shampoo). Let this sit on the stain for 5 minutes before soaking in cool water for 30 minutes, then gently rinse in cool water. Handwash in cool water following the fabric care instructions.

If you really don't want to wash your silk item (for example, if it's a tie), try rubbing alcohol. Test it on a hidden area first as rubbing alcohol can damage or discolour delicate fabrics. If possible, place a clean, absorbent cloth under the stained area, and working from the reverse, apply rubbing alcohol directly to the stain using a cotton ball or cloth. Dab gently (don't rub) to push the stain into the cloth beneath and work from the outside of the stain towards the centre. Rinse with cold water and wash the item following care instructions.

Wool and cashmere

For wool or cashmere, wet the stained area with lukewarm water and gently rub it in netted gall soap or a mild detergent or baby shampoo, depending on the stain (see page 90). Soak the whole garment in lukewarm water using a few drops of a mild eco detergent or baby shampoo. Swirl and gently squeeze the suds through the fabric, then leave it to sit for 10 minutes. Rinse thoroughly in clean lukewarm water, gently squeezing out the water by hand. Remove the excess water by laying the garment in a towel and rolling it up, then smooth it back into its original shape and place it flat on a towel to dry naturally, away from heat or sunlight (never tumble dry). When dry, use a cool iron over a clean cloth to press the garment or use a clothes steamer, if you have one.

You can get most tannin stains out of robust fabrics that tolerate hot temperatures, such as linen or cotton, by pouring boiling or near-boiling water directly on to the stain, then laundering according to the care instructions.

Carpets – wool, wool mix and synthetic

Carpets require special attention because trying to clean with too much water will leave a stubborn watermark (and you can't throw a carpet into the washing machine to rinse out all the stain-removal agents). Excess water can also seep into the carpet, reaching the underlay, which will be difficult to dry, leading to mould and mildew. It really pays to apply your cleaning solution using a spray bottle as this avoids the tendency to over-wet. Another common mistake is to rub a carpet rather than dab. Dabbing will preserve the carpet's texture (plus, rubbing the stain can push the stain deep into the fibres). Once dry, vacuum to restore the pile.

• Fresh and dried red wine stains on wool or wool-mix carpets
(or if you don't know what your carpet is made from)
This is every party-thrower's biggest nightmare and the trigger for many insurance claims. If you act quickly, you should be able to remove a big red wine spill. There are two methods that work well. Whichever you use, remember to dab, not rub and that patience really does pay off.

Method One: Gently blot red wine with an absorbent white cloth or kitchen paper. Pour white wine over the stain and blot again with the absorbent cloth. Dilute ½ teaspoon of washing-up liquid in 250ml of warm water and dab it on to stain. Rinse the solution by dabbing with clean cool water, but don't over-soak. Leave to dry. Vacuum to restore the pile.

Method Two: Spray neat white vinegar on to the stain. Immediately sprinkle 1 tablespoon of bicarb on top and let it fizz. Brush off the bicarb with a dustpan and brush. Dab with a damp, clean cloth, then dab it with a tiny squirt of washing-up liquid diluted in cool water, then dab with clean water. Leave to dry. Vacuum to restore the pile.

• *Fresh and dried red wine stains on synthetic carpets*
Blot with a clean, absorbent cloth (do not rub). Make up a solution of ¼ teaspoon of oxygen bleach in 300ml of warm water with ¼ teaspoon of washing-up liquid, pour it into a spray bottle and swirl gently to dissolve the oxygen bleach. Spray the stain and leave for 15 minutes. Dab with an absorbent cloth. Then remove the residue of solution by dabbing again with a clean, damp cloth. Leave to dry. Repeat as necessary, then vacuum to restore the pile. *Remember the solution remains active only for 6 hours.*

• *Fresh and dried pet-pee stains on wool or wool-mix carpets*
(or if you don't know what your carpet is made from)
If the stain is still fresh, you should be able to remove it with white vinegar and water. Blot the stain with kitchen paper or a dry tea towel to soak up as much as possible. Spritz with a 50/50 mix of white vinegar and water, followed by a sprinkling of bicarb while the vinegar solution is still wet. Let it fizz, then remove the bicarb with a dustpan and brush. To rinse, spray water on to the mark and dab with a clean, absorbent cloth. Repeat as necessary. This last step is important, as leaving the bicarb/vinegar solution to dry on the carpet can result in a white patch.

The method for dried stains is almost the same, but first dampen the stain by spritzing with water, leave for 5 minutes, then blot with a piece of kitchen paper. Follow the method for a fresh pet-pee stain but spritz with neat white vinegar (rather than the diluted solution), followed by the sprinkle of bicarb. Again, leave to fizz and remove with a dustpan and brush. Finish by spraying water again and dabbing with a clean, absorbent cloth.

- **Fresh and dried pet-pee stains on synthetic carpets**
Follow the same method for wool and wool-mix carpets, but instead
of spraying with white vinegar and water, make up an oxygen-bleach
solution (2 tablespoons oxygen bleach to 1 litre warm water). Once
dry, vacuum to restore the pile.

- **Fresh and dried poo and vomit on wool and wool mix carpets**
(or if you don't know what your carpet is made from)
Gently scrape off the debris with a spoon or knife. If the stain has
dried, slightly re-wet by spraying with water. Sprinkle bicarb on
to the stain and leave it to soak in for 15 minutes to neutralise smells
and help lift out the acidic compounds in vomit and faeces. Blot
with a damp cloth. Rub gall soap over a damp sponge to produce
a lather, then dab the stain with the sponge, working inwards from
the outside edge and being careful not to over-wet. Dab with a
clean, damp cloth to rinse. Once dry, vacuum to restore the pile.

- **Fresh and dried poo and vomit on synthetic carpets**
Gently scrape off the debris with a spoon or knife, and if the stain
has dried re-wet by spraying lightly with water. Use a mild solution
of oxygen bleach (1 tablespoon oxygen bleach to 500ml warm
water), leaving it to work on the stain for 30 minutes. Dab with a
clean, damp cloth to rinse. Once dry, vacuum to restore the pile.

- **Fresh and dried mud stains on any carpets**
Let the stain dry. Scrape off the debris with a spoon or knife.
Mix 3 parts bicarb to roughly 1 part water to form a paste that's
the consistency of toothpaste (always do a spot test on a hidden
area as the bicarb may bleach the carpet). Apply the paste to the
mud stain and leave it for 2 hours or more, until dry; then vacuum.
Dab with a clean, damp cloth to rinse. Once dry, vacuum again
to restore the pile.

• **_Chocolate on carpets and upholstery_** _(works on all types of stains and fabric)_

On carpets, especially, it is worth using a spray bottle containing a mild detergent solution. Spritz (don't over-wet) the stain and dab with a clean, dry cloth. Rubbing alcohol is good for removing chocolate stains from upholstery, in particular, because there is less risk of a watermark forming.

Leave the chocolate to dry. Scrape off any excess; do not rub. Gently dab the stain with a damp kitchen paper or a damp cloth. Spray rubbing alcohol on to the stain and, working from the outside towards the middle of the stain, gently dab with a clean tea towel or white cloth. Repeat for as long as you can see the chocolate coming off. If you are unfortunate enough to get a watermark, see our tip on how to remove it on page 135.

WHEN A CARPET STAIN PERSISTS

When you have a persistent stain on a synthetic carpet, first spritz the stain with a little water, then sprinkle some soda crystals directly on to the damp patch, leave it for 10 minutes, then vacuum. If that doesn't work, mix 1 tablespoon of soda crystals with 500ml of warm water. Sponge a little of the solution into the stain, and blot – don't rub. Rinse with a damp cloth and dab dry. For wool/wool mix carpets or where you are not sure what the carpet is made of, spritz with a little water, then apply gall soap, gently dabbing, and rinse thoroughly with water without over-wetting. Dab dry. Vacuum the carpet to restore the pile.

Watermark stains on upholstery

It can be infuriating to get a stain off your sofa, only to be left with a watermark instead. If the covers are washable, a launder will normally remove it. If the upholstery is fitted, spray distilled water sparingly around the watermark without soaking the fabric and leave it for 5 minutes to soften the stain. Wrap a clean, soft cloth around your finger, dip it in white vinegar and gently dab the edges of the watermark. Start at the outer edge and work towards the centre. Once the mark has gone, it is important to then lightly spray the whole surface with distilled water again to stop a second watermark appearing. Now use a hairdryer on a low setting, running it evenly over the whole area. You may need to repeat the process for the best results.

OUT AND ABOUT

Rubbing alcohol doubles up as a great instant stain remedy on clothes if you are out and about. We carry a small spray bottle in our bags. It is particularly good for grease, chocolate, ink and lipstick stains. Blot off any excess, then spray on the rubbing alcohol and dab, dab, dab with a white cloth – you will see the stain transferring on to the cloth. White wine is also good for fresh red wine stains on natural fibres. Blot the red wine, then pour a small amount of white wine over the stain and blot again. These methods will start to break down your stains, so that you can deal with them properly once you get home.

PLUNDER THE DRINKS TROLLEY

Sometimes you can find the best emergency cleaning ingredients in the most unexpected places. These spirited solutions can be another great first port of call until you have more time.

Fizzy water/soda water: This is great for lifting red wine stains out of fabric or carpets, particularly those made of synthetic material. The carbonic acid that forms the bubbles in sparkling water helps to break down red-wine residue, and the bubbles themselves help lift the stain out. Blot away as much wine as possible, before pouring some fizzy water on to the fresh stain – let it fizz and then blot with a clean cloth. Sometimes this is all you need to do.

White wine: At the start of this chapter, we cautioned against people automatically sloshing white wine on to red-wine spills. This is because it only works well on a wool carpet and generally as a first step. Just pour and blot, then blot again with clean water. Don't use white wine on synthetic carpet (that's a job for oxygen bleach, see page 128).

Sparkling wine or Champagne: Again, this is one for wool carpets only. The fizzing action of the bubbles helps dislodge the stains, especially on tea or coffee stains. Pour a small amount on to the stain, leave it to fizz and then blot.

Vodka: A naturally colourless and odourless deodoriser, vodka is good for greasy stains. Gently blot the grease mark with the vodka, then rinse it with cool water.

Gin: This is good for grease and ink stains. Pour a little gin on to a white cloth, blot (don't rub) the stain, then rinse with water.

Lemons: To whiten and brighten and attack rust stains, lemon juice squeezed directly on to the stain, then left to sit for 5 minutes and rinsed with water is pure magic.

Ice cubes: Put these in a plastic bag and press them on to chewing gum to make it brittle and easy to scrape off. The process also works to remove candle wax from walls, floors, rug and carpets.

Salt: All good drinks trolleys have salt on them for the margaritas don't they? You can use the salt to soak up wine, blood and grease on both carpets and upholstery. Sprinkle salt on to the damp stain and leave it to sit for 20 minutes. Vacuum or brush away the salt, then continue the stain-removal process. If you're dealing with cotton clothes, sprinkle a generous amount of table salt on to the fresh stain, leave it for 1 hour, then launder.

CHAPTER FOUR

The Power of Scent

We both love essential oils — for us, the whole process of cleaning is so much more fun if we can whizz around with a spray bottle, spreading glorious natural scents. As a result, these essential oils have become integral to the Purdy & Figg brand. However, you absolutely don't need to add essential oils to your cleaning recipes — you can clean the house from top to bottom perfectly well using natural minerals that are scent-free.

Our mission, when it comes to scent, is completely different to that of 'Big Clean' — which pushes out punchy, acrid and sometimes eye-wateringly strong fragrances. We are vehemently opposed to the idea that a home that knocks you over with its smell of bleach, pine or artificial flowers equals an admirably clean one. If you follow our methods, you simply won't need all those super-scented cleaning products, and definitely not an air-freshener plugged into every possible electric socket.

Why smell matters

The truth is that there's nothing more reassuring than the familiar smell of home. For Charlotte, who lives on the outskirts of a village in the Chilterns, home smells of wood smoke, floor polish and rush matting. For Purdy, who lives on the Suffolk coast, it's the crisp, faintly sulphuric sea air mixed with the scent of lavender from her favourite diffuser in the hallway. In their different ways, these familiar home smells signal safety and calm for both of us.

The human physical and psychological reactions to smell are deeply rooted in our survival instincts. In the first few years of life, we build a library of smells that becomes hardwired. We learn to associate different smells with danger and safety, and with edible and toxic or spoiled food, as well as with places, people and emotions, which we are then able to gauge on a sliding scale of how pleasant or unpleasant they are. This is known as odour hedonic perception. Smell is the most powerful trigger of the senses for memory recall, and it affects cognition, concentration and stress levels. Tiny molecules in the air go straight to the olfactory receptors in our nose to be assessed by our limbic system – the part of the brain that governs memory, behaviour and emotions – and this in turn influences our mood. Our cultural background, genes, age, health and gender, not to mention the concentration of the odour itself, will all have significant impacts on our individual perception and response.

All that said, it's worth remembering that when we are exposed to any smell for a prolonged period, we quickly become nose blind and stop noticing it. Ask a smoker if their house smells of cigarette smoke and they'll almost certainly say it does when they come home, but not an hour later. This is because our brains process the olfactory information simply in order to work out whether it signals danger. If we like a smell, we can safely ignore it until it changes to something else, or there is a break, and the same smell is picked up again later. This natural adaptation allows us to sniff out potentially harmful smells like burning or gas.

Incidentally, don't ever be fooled into thinking that the best way to deal with a bad smell is to try and cover it up, whether with essential oils, a scented candle, air freshener or something else. You need to get rid of a bad smell, not disguise it. This could mean anything from opening the window to let in fresh air, to calling the plumber or simply disposing of some offending article. There are tips and tricks on banishing bad smells on pages 64, 67 and 77.

Scent wars

Have you noticed that when you go anywhere near the cleaning aisle of a supermarket, there's often an overwhelming smell coming from all those detergents, laundry products and air fresheners? It's as if we're living in a loop of escalating scent wars, with 'Big Clean' developing ever-stronger smells in a bid for our custom, based on the marketing gambit that the stronger the smell, the more likely we are to buy it. Research by Professor Charles Spence[xxvii], a cognitive neuroscientist interested in multi-sensory design, has suggested that adding the appropriate fragrance to a laundry detergent can convince us that our clothes feel softer.

Well, not all of us. In our view, most synthetically scented cleaning products do not smell at all nice, especially those fabric conditioners trying to replicate exotic-sounding combinations like pomegranates and crushed silk.

'Probably one of my most telling childhood memories is of coming downstairs in the morning and finding the Paisley tablecloth still there from dinner the night before, and a delicious smell of old cigar smoke and undrunk wine and coffee and so forth. I remember as a young kid, sensing that something good had been going on and that I was missing out.'

Fergus Henderson, Chef, cited in *Home: What Our Homes Really Mean to Us* by Stafford Cliff

Introducing essential oils

Back in the early days of Purdy & Figg, we both enrolled on an aromatherapy course to learn more about essential oils, including their fascinating health benefits. We learnt that just inhaling them can help boost our mood and concentration, reduce stress and even improve sleep. Some have mild antimicrobial properties, too. If you're making your own cleaning products, as we hope you will, you'll find it's great fun to experiment with making your own signature blends of essential oils too. We are convinced that using them helps to create a relaxing ambience, whether they are diffused as a room scent, placed as pulse points around the home or added to your cleaning products (see Chapter 2).

What are they?

Essential oils are highly fragranced, concentrated liquids consisting of volatile chemical compounds extracted from various plant parts, such as citrus-fruit rinds, flowers, twigs, leaves and needles, seeds, roots, resins and bark. Plants create these substances either to protect themselves from disease or attack or to attract pollinators. And since a typical essential oil contains 100 or more chemical constituents, some of which are not even identifiable, it is extremely difficult to replicate their unique scent synthetically.

How to create your favourite blends

To create a complex scent that evolves over time, we recommend blending top-, middle- and base-note essential oils together, rather than going for one. Top- (or head-) note essential oils give an instant hit of scent but evaporate fast; middle-note (or heart-note) essential oils are the ones that add body to a blend; while base-note essential oils are the couch potatoes that will keep going for hours and even days.

Over the page is a list of our favourite oils, with their respective notes included. We usually refer to them by their common names – for example, 'lemon' (instead of *Citrus x limon*), but we have provided their botanical names here so that you know exactly what you need to buy, as there are many varieties of plants with similar common names. For example, there are more than four types of cedarwood essential oil, among which Atlas cedarwood (*Cedrus atlantica*) is globally endangered, whereas red cedar (*Juniperus virginiana*) is not.

Essential oils

TOP NOTES

EUCALYPTUS PEPPERMINT (*Eucalyptus dives*):
herbaceous, woody and minty.

LEMON* (*Citrus x limon*): citrusy, uplifting and stimulating.

MANDARIN (*Citrus reticulata*): gentle, calming and uplifting.

PETITGRAIN* (*Citrus aurantium* var. *amara*):
floral, green, calming and balancing.

SPEARMINT (*Mentha spicata*):
minty fresh and uplifting (use sparingly).

SWEET ORANGE (*Citrus sinensis*): citrusy and uplifting.

SWEET BASIL (*Ocimium basilicum*):
herbaceous and energising (use sparingly).

TEA TREE (*Melaleuca alternifolia*):
leafy/woody, medicinal and uplifting.

WHITE GRAPEFRUIT (*Citrus x paradisi*):
citrusy, tangy and uplifting.

**These essential oils not only provide fragrance,
but also have deodorising properties.*

MIDDLE NOTES

CLARYSAGE* (*Salvia sclarea*): sweet, herbaceous and uplifting.

CORIANDER SEED (*Coriandrum sativum*): spicy and calming.

GERANIUM* (*Pelargonium graveolens*): floral and balancing.

LAVANDIN (*Lavandula x intermedia*): floral, calming and uplifting.

LAVENDER* (*Lavandula angustifolia*): floral and calming.

ROMAN CHAMOMILE (*Chamaemelum nobile*):
sweet, herbaceous and soothing.

YLANG YLANG Complete (*Cananga odorata*):
exotic floral and relaxing (middle/base note).

BASE NOTES

BENZOIN* (*Styrax benzoin*): warm, vanilla-like and calming.

PATCHOULI* (*Pogostemon cablin*): relaxing, deep and dreamy,
and reminds some of us of Afghan coats and hippy beads.

VIRGINIAN CEDARWOOD (*Juniperus virginiana*):
woody and calming.

YLANG YLANG Complete (*Cananga odorata*):
exotic floral and relaxing (middle/base note).

While our Clever Clean recipes (see pages 56–9) don't need essential oils, we think adding them elevates cleaning from a chore to a pleasure – it becomes not only about making your home spick and span, but about going some way to refreshing the soul. Here are some of our favourite blends to get you started. But do experiment until you find combinations you love. (Incidentally, powerful-smelling essential oils, such as sweet basil, ylang-ylang, spearmint and tea tree, work best when used sparingly.)

For the multi-surface spray (see page 56)

Blend 1: 10 drops of sweet orange and 10 drops of pink grapefruit.

Blend 2: 5 drops of sweet orange, 5 drops of pink grapefruit, 7 drops of geranium and 3 drops of ylang ylang (as a general rule, use ylang ylang sparingly).

Blend 3: 11 drops of lavender (this is a classic, great on its own and blends well with other essential oils), 6 drops of geranium and 3 drops of ylang ylang.

Blend 4: 12 drops of pink grapefruit, 5 drops of geranium and 3 drops of patchouli (which makes for a deep, dreamy aroma).

For the window, mirror and glass cleaner (see page 57)
10 drops of lemon – this is lovely just on its own.

For the gentle abrasive scrub paste (see page 58)

8 drops of white grapefruit, 8 drops of lavender or lavandin and 4 drops of tea tree.

For the loo cleaner (see page 59)

Blend 1: 14 drops of lemon; 11 drops of white grapefruit and 5 drops of lavender or lavandin.

Blend 2: 4 drops of sweet basil, 11 drops of spearmint and 15 drops of lavender, lavandin or lemon.

CONSTANCE AND CHARLIE'S MIDSUMMER FLORAL WEDDING BLEND

Creating an essential oil blend for celebrations, such as a wedding, is a lovely thing to do. When Purdy's son Charlie announced he was getting married, he and his fiancée asked us to create a unique blend to diffuse at the ceremony and the reception. Constance wanted a fresh, floral smell suggestive of midsummer, so we made a blend using lavender, neroli and lemon. They use it at home to this day as an evocative reminder of their very special occasion. Talk about scent memories...

Simple home scents

Along with adding essential oils to your natural cleaning products, you might want to consider other ways to let the scent of essential oils linger in your home. Our favourite 'low-fi' methods are scented reed diffusers and room sprays, both of which are easy to make and fun to blend; we like to place bottles with reed diffusers in special spots, which give an instant hit as we walk past and are especially effective in small spaces like bathrooms or on tables in rooms near the door.

But there are many other ways of dispersing essential oils into the air, from old-school tea-light burners to the most sophisticated ultrasonic electric diffusers, remote controlled via an App, allowing diffusion to start before you step inside.

The safest, most effective method is through intermittent rather than continuous diffusion, by which we mean 30–45 minutes of diffusion followed by a 30–45-minute break. As we explained, we eventually stop noticing smells, so an electric diffuser permanently going full blast in the home becomes little more than a pollutant and research suggests it may also put unnecessary stress on the body. We have been working closely on this with Margaret Karlinski, our in-house aromatherapist; and, based on three decades of studying essential oils, she is firmly of the view that less is more, and that we should use scent sparingly. She even advises us to 'de-scent' our spaces from time to time. Remember, it's the moment you open that door or drawer or walk past that room that gives you the hit.

Margaret's room spray

This gorgeous, easy-to-make spray is a lovely way to refresh a room, revive a piece of clothing without having to launder it or make your own drawer and shelf liners. Combine 250ml ethanol (94.5%) –

which, unlike rubbing alcohol, has no smell – with 1 teaspoon of either lavender or geranium essential oil or a mixture of both, and pour the blend into a clean, dry 250ml glass spray bottle. Spray liberally upwards and towards the centre of rooms or directly on to sheets, towels, beds, carpets, bathroom mats and clothes. A few spritzes from 15cm distance or more will avoid marks on light fabrics. The spray is almost colourless, so won't stain, but if you are concerned about colour fastness, test on a hidden area first. For drawer liners, spray A2 sheets of blotting paper. The alcohol will evaporate quickly, but the scent of the essential oils will linger.
SHELF LIFE: 1 YEAR

Margaret's reed and diffuser blend

Blend a teaspoon each of lemon or sweet orange, geranium and patchouli essential oils with 250ml of reed-diffuser solvent base, such as Augeo Multi Clean, also known as Augeo Diffuser Base (see Key Suppliers and Products, page 165). Transfer the mixture into a narrow-necked bottle and add 10–12 reeds, which might take a while to absorb the mixture. Leave them for a few minutes and turn them upside down. After a few days, turn the reeds upside down again. Thicker reeds work well as they have a larger evaporation area. As the blend will colour the reeds, we prefer black ones. Always protect polished or painted surfaces as spills and drips may damage them.

Diffusion in children's bedrooms

We recommend only lavender or Roman chamomile before bedtime in children's rooms, or mandarin to help settle a grizzly child – and only 1–2 drops in each case. Ultrasonic diffusers are good, as they automatically switch off if they are accidentally knocked over.

SAFETY, SUSTAINABILITY AND ADULTERATION

Essential oils are skin irritants and can cause allergic reactions.

- Beware of any room-spray recipes that mix essential oils with water, because without a preservative, bacteria will breed in water within days, so always stick to ethanol.

- Always place diffusers out of reach of children and pets.

- Make sure pets can leave any room where essential oils are being diffused and never diffuse in a room with a caged animal or bird.

- Always buy from reputable suppliers. Organic certification is a good choice but can be pricey.

- Essential oils should be sold and stored in dark glass – never plastic bottles because the oils can degrade from heat and sunlight.

- Unusually low prices may be a sign of adulteration or poor quality and beware any mention of 'Fragrance Oil', 'Essence' or 'Perfume' on the bottle or label.

- Beware of dubious marketing claims, such as 'genuine essential oil', 'therapeutic grade', 'aromatherapy grade', or other phrases such as 'nature identical', 'reconstituted', 'lavender 40:42', because these are unlikely to be pure essential oils.

- Endangered species to avoid include rosewood and Indian or Mysore sandalwood. For more information about endangered species and conservation, visit The International Union for Conservation of Nature IUCN.org.

Other natural ways to scent the home

If essential oils are not for you, there are plenty of sweet-smelling alternatives. Indoor flowering bulbs are a wonderful way to bring scent indoors during winter and early spring: bowls of paperwhite narcissi or fragrant white hyacinths work well, and you can stagger their planting to give you 4 months of scent and colour from December onwards. From early summer, scented leaf pelargoniums look wonderfully fresh and if you pinch the leaves as you pass by, you get an uplifting burst of scent. Bowls of pot pourri sound old-fashioned, but if you choose our favourite from Santa Maria Novella, you get a subtle, balsamic scent reminiscent of cool churches on hot summer days. You can also harvest your own lavender flowers at the end of summer if you have any bushes growing outside. Dry them on newspaper for a couple of weeks, then strip the stalks of flowers, putting them in small muslin squares tied up with ribbon. It's lovely to open up drawers and cupboards in which you store your clothes, bedlinen and towels and be greeted by a soft lavender smell.

Create your own magic sit spot

And finally, now that you're an expert at making your own natural scents and knowing how to use them, you just need to create what Charlotte calls a 'magic sit spot' – or two if you can: one inside your home and one outside. These are places to sit undisturbed and unobserved, reading a book or having a long phone conversation. It's where no one can find you. Indoors, there is probably a wall behind you and something nice to look at in front: a view outside or a picture you like – and the best way of rounding it off is, of course, a lovely scent.

OUR MISSION

When we told our friends we were thinking of writing a book about cleaning and cleaning products, many of them looked at us as if we were slightly unhinged. It was one thing to set up a company selling cleaning products, but quite another to write a whole book about them, or at least one that was interesting.

Sometimes, at odd moments when we felt really stuck — like when Purdy was testing a stain remedy for the sixth time or trying to simplify the explanation for how to mix oxygen bleach — we thought perhaps we *were* unhinged. We certainly felt it occasionally.

But now that we've finished this book and it's tangible, we can look back and reflect on how much we've learnt in the process, from deepening our knowledge of microplastics, minerals and the microbiome, to making new discoveries about the world of scent. We've better understood the importance of just getting it done, whatever it is, and the fundamental rule to keep it simple.

From those early days of experimenting together in a garage, we have grown into a rapidly expanding business with central London offices and our own factory — our names over the door — which makes us immensely proud and a little awestruck. We are part of a big team now, our roles changing so fast that we even have to make appointments to speak to each other.

Yet we never lose sight of what compelled us to start Purdy & Figg in the first place and which remains our mission today: to inspire you to rethink how you clean your home and the products you use in it — even if it's just switching your washing-up liquid or your loo cleaner. Of course, we very much hope that you'll have a stab at making all your own natural cleaning products and try our stain-removal remedies, too, and see how fun, simple and doable it all is.

Above all, we hope that our guide guides you, and that you will come to regard this book as a trusted friend, its pages getting faded and worn with use, and their wisdom passed on for generations to come.

THE CLEVER CLEANING CALENDAR

Here's our round-the-year to-do list, intended to inspire you to get on and start eating the whale. Do just one task a week — whatever it is — and you'll be amazed at how much you can achieve over the course of 12 months. All the recipes, hacks and advice you'll need are included in this book — though bear in mind our list is not definitive. Rather, it is made up of suggestions and ideas to get you going.

March

We start here because spring has arrived – and it's a hopeful month. Get windows sparkling and stop moths in their tracks.

Week 1: Clean windows inside – tackle a room at a time.

Week 2: Dust and spritz blinds, launder or green clean curtains.

Week 3: Deep clean just one room, wardrobe or cupboard. If you do one a month that's twelve in a year.

Week 4: Prepare your natural moth balls and store your winter clothes.

April

The clocks have gone forward; the days are getting longer and it's time to get your outdoors ready.

Week 1: Wipe down outdoor furniture, clean the decking and get the laundry line up.

Week 2: Descale the shower fixture, taps and grouting in the bathroom.

Week 3: Treat your washing machine and dishwasher to a lovely deodorising deep clean.

Week 4: Deep clean another room or cupboard.

May

Summer beckons, and along with salads and sunshine, moths and ants are preparing to invade.

Week 1: Check sell-by dates on dry foods in the kitchen cupboard, chuck out-of-date foods and spritz clean shelves to deter hungry insects and invaders.

Week 2: Defrost the freezer and deep clean the fridge.

Week 3: Treat pillows, bed covers and winter duvets to a 'green' clean at the laundry.

Week 4: Deep clean another room or cupboard.

June

Get ready for BBQ season and give your oven a break.

Week 1: Out comes the BBQ, and time to give those grubby oven racks a deep clean.

Week 2: Declutter desks and your home office; chuck out redundant paperwork and files.

Week 3: Sort through books you will never read again and take them to the charity shop or leave them on the front garden wall for passers-by to help themselves.

Week 4: Dust down the remaining books and bookshelves.

July

Make the most of the dry, sunny days and launder bulky pet bedding.

Week 1: Wash pet bedding and washable rugs, and dry them outdoors.

Week 2: Time to clean some more windows.

Week 3: Dust behind the radiators.

Week 4: Deep clean another room or cupboard. You're getting there...

August

Take a holiday. Lie in a deckchair. Read a novel. Relax, but don't forget to order indoor and spring flowering bulbs.

September

The days are still long and may be golden, so make hay while the sun is still shining.

Week 1: Plant indoor bulbs to flower and scent your home from Christmas to January.

Week 2: Check out the medicine cupboard or first-aid box and chuck out-of-date items. Order candles and matches for the months ahead.

Week 3: Steam clean or polish hard floors.

Week 4: Deep clean another room or cupboard.

October

The first frosts are the herald of winter; the nights are long and it's time to dig out your cold-weather kit.

Week 1: Put away summer clothes, bring out warm coats and winter woolies, spritz cleaning cupboards and drawers as you go.

Week 2: Away with the BBQ, outdoor furniture and the laundry line.

Week 3: Time to declutter desks and home offices again. Paperwork accumulates fast.

Week 4: Descale the shower fixtures and taps and clean the grouting in the bathroom.

November

Christmas is looming, so get planning now and prepare for hibernation-style sleeping and comfort.

Week 1: Flip mattresses.

Week 2: Treat your washing machine and dishwasher to a lovely deodorising deep clean.

Week 3: Prepare rooms for family and friends coming for Christmas.

Week 4: Deep clean another room or cupboard.

December

Take this month off too, as you'll be so busy with everything else, you'll barely have time to do much more than the basics.

January

It's a hunker-down month when everything seems to stop, but the sight of the first snowdrop shows that the seasons are turning beneath your feet, so keep going.

Week 1: Declutter one room and take surplus nick nacks and unwanted Christmas presents to the recycling centre or charity shop.

Week 2: Descale the iron, kettle and loo.

Week 3: Defrost the freezer and deep clean the fridge.

Week 4: Deep clean another room or cupboard.

February

The low rays of watery spring sunshine show in merciless detail the state of your windows and dusty corners where the spiders have been busy.

Week 1: Clean light fittings, dust down lampshades and check lightbulbs are clean and working.

Week 2: Have a corner and cobweb blitz, but remind yourself that spiders eat flies and aphids, so they have been working in your service.

Week 3: Dust those dark corners.

Week 4: Deep clean another room or cupboard.

REFERENCES

p.18 [i] How our cleaning brands are helping people cope with Covid-19 [www.unilever.com/news/news-search/2020/how-our-cleaning-brands-are-helping-people-cope-with-covid-19/]

p.19 [ii] The farm-like effect: rural exposures in early life, the microbiome, and asthma [www.jacionline.org/article/S0091-6749(21)00661-8/fulltext]

p.20 [iii] Antibacterial household products: cause for concern [wwwnc.cdc.gov/eid/article/7/7/01-7705_article]

and

Antibacterial cleaning products and drug resistance [https://pmc.ncbi.nlm.nih.gov/articles/PMC3366732/#:~:text=Concern%20is%20growing%20over%20the,resistance%20(1%E2%80%933)]

p.20 [iv] Too clean or not too clean: the hygiene hypothesis and home hygiene [https://pmc.ncbi.nlm.nih.gov/articles/PMC1448690/]

p. 21 [v] Volatile organic compounds emitted by conventional and 'green' cleaning products in the U.S. market [www.sciencedirect.com/science/article/pii/S0045653523018374?via%3Dihub]

p.21 [vi] Cleaning at home and at work in relation to lung function decline and airway obstruction [www.atsjournals.org/doi/10.1164/rccm.201706-1311OC]

p. 23 [vii] Widely used benzalkonium chloride disinfectants can promote antibiotic resistance. [https://journals.asm.org/doi/10.1128/aem.01201-18]

p. 23 [viii] Exposure effects of benzalkonium chloride (BAC) on gonadal physiology and fertility suppression in medaka (Oryzias latipes) [www.sciencedirect.com/science/article/abs/pii/S0269749124014921#:~:text=BAC%20exposure%20results%20in%20enlarged,autophagic%20gene%20expression%20in%20medaka]

p.23 [ix] Phthalate exposure and breast cancer incidence [https://pmc.ncbi.nlm.nih.gov/articles/PMC7351345/#:~:text=Phthalates%20are%20potential%20endocrine%20disruptors,16%2D18%20and%20some%20cancers.&text=Preclinical%20evidence%20suggests%20that%20some,estrogen%20receptor%20(ER)%20signaling]

p.23 [x] Breast Cancer UK: The cocktail effect [www.breastccanceruk.org.uk/reduce-your-risk/chemicals-and-our-environment/endocrine-system-and-edcs/]

p.23 [xi] Dangers of mixing bleach with cleaners [https://doh.wa.gov/community-and-environment/contaminants/bleach-mixing-dangers#:~:text=Mixing%20Bleach%20and%20Ammonia,Nausea]

p. 25 [xii] The contribution of household chemicals to environmental discharges via effluents [www.sciencedirect.com/science/article/abs/pii/S0301479714006021]

p.25 [xiii] Household waste statistics [www.wrap.ngo/media-centre/press-releases/households-waste-over-one-billion-items-every-year-could-be-recycled]

p.26 [xiv] Burned: why incineration is harmful [www.nrdc.org/bio/daniel-rosenberg/burned-why-waste-incineration-harmful]

p26 [xv] Plastic pollution: facts and figures [www.sas.org.uk/plastic-pollution/plastic-pollution-facts-figures/]
and
Fighting for trash-free seas [https://oceanconservancy.org/trash-free-seas/plastics-in-the-ocean/]

p. 26 [xvi] 240,000 tiny pieces of plastic in a one litre bottle of water [www.nih.gov/news-events/nih-research-matters/plastic-particles-bottled-water]
and
Nanoplastics in bottles water [www.pnas.org/doi/10.1073/pnas.2300582121]

p.26 [xvii] Your brain is full of microplastics: are they harming you? [https://www.nature.com/articles/d41586-025-00405-8]

p.27 [xviii] Appearance of microplastics in the environment [https://pmc.ncbi.nlm.nih.gov/articles/PMC9920460/]

p.27 [xix] The Great Pacific Garbage Patch [https://theoceancleanup.com/great-pacific-garbage-patch/]

p.32 [xx] Calories burned doing housework [www.verywellfit.com/how-to-burn-more-calories-cleaning-house-3495596]

p.39 [xxi] Ten most hated household chores [www.tapwarehouse.com/blog/latest-news/uk-cleaning-habits-report#Housework---who-is-doing-more-chores?]

p.45 [xxii] Where citric acid comes from [https://pmc.ncbi.nlm.nih.gov/articles/PMC3769771]

p.47 [xxiii] Cleaning complaints about the other half [www.tapwarehouse.com/blog/latest-news/uk-cleaning-habits-report#Housework---who-is-doing-more-chores?]

p. 82 [xxiv] Flies as pollinators [https://www.annualreviews.org/content/journals/10.1146/annurev-ento-011019-025055]

p. 85 [xxv] Mango farmers and carcasses [www.smithsonianmag.com/science-nature/how-much-do-flies-help-pollination-180977177/]

p.91 [xxvi] Smithsonian Institute: stain removal [https://mci.si.edu/stain-removal]

p.142 [xxvii] Sensing the future. www.aqr.org.uk/a/20080228-future

BIBLIOGRAPHY

Superwoman: Every Woman's Book of Household Management, Shirley Conran (Sidgwick & Jackson, 1975)

Down with Superwoman! Everything You Need to Know about Running a Home, Shirley Conran (Penguin, 1991)

Spit and Polish: Old fashioned ways to banish dirt dust and decay, Lucy Lethbridge, (Bloomsbury, 2016)

What Our Homes Really Mean to Us, Stafford Cliff (Quadrille, 2006)

Never Home Alone: From Microbes to Millipedes, Camel Crickets, and Honeybees, the Natural History of Where We Live, Rob Dunn (Basic Books, 2018)

KEY SUPPLIERS AND PRODUCTS

We do not receive payment from companies mentioned in this book. Many of the products listed below are available via Amazon and eBay, but we like to support independent, ethical suppliers and hardware stores when we can. The following suggestions are not definitive, they are products we have tried and liked. You can also head to our website, clevercleaning.co.uk

Bicarbonate of Soda (Bicarb)
Dri-Pak (dri-pak.co.uk). This brand is available at hardware shops including B&Q, Robert Dyas and online retailers that supply ethically sourced products such as Big Green Smile (biggreensmile.com) and Ethical Superstore (www.ethicalsuperstore.com)

Brushes
Cape Cod Horsehair Brush (amazon.co.uk)
Leather Repair Company (leatherrepaircompany.com)

Castile Soap (Bar)
Dr Bronner (drbronner.co.uk)

Castile Soap (Liquid)
Aromantics (aromantic.co.uk)
The Soapery (thesoapery.co.uk)

Cedar Balls
Lakeland (lakeland.com)

Citric Acid
Dri-Pak (dri-pak.co.uk). See note for Bicarb, above.

Cleaning Blocks
Big Green Smile (biggreensmile.com)
Amazon (amazon.co.uk)

Diffusers
Florihana Microparticle Diffuser (florihana.com)
Aromatherapy Associates (aromatherapyassociates.com)
Quinessence (quinessence.com)
Oshadhi (oshadhi.co.uk)

Distilled Water
Available in hardware shops and most supermarkets, and via Amazon (amazon.co.uk)

Drain Cleaning
Ecodoo Drain Cleaner available at Big Green Smile (biggreensmile.com)
Drain Snake (Vastar) on Amazon: (amazon.co.uk)

Essential Oils
Absolute Aromas (absolute-aromas.com)
Florihana (florihana.com)
Neal's Yard (nealsyardremedies.com)
Oshadhi (oshadhi.co.uk)
Quinessence (quinessence.com)

Fer a Cheval Stain Removing Marseille Soap Bar
French Soaps (www.frenchsoaps.co.uk)

Gall Stain Bar Soap and Liquid Soap
Sonett Gall Soap (Bar and Liquid) (sonett.eu)
Heitmann Gall Soap Bar and Liquid Soap (amazon.co.uk)
Disana Liquid Gall Soap for Wool (thenappylady.co.uk)

Glass bottles and trigger sprays
G Baldwins & Co (baldwins.co.uk)
Ampulla Ltd (ampulla.co.uk)

Horsehair Brush
Cape Cod Horsehair Brush (amazon.co.uk)
Leather Repair Company Horse Hair Brush (leatherrepaircompany.com)

Kilner Jars
Lakeland (lakeland.co.uk)
Robert Dyas (robertdyas.co.uk)

Laundry Brush – see Horsehair Brush

Liquid Detergent – see Laundry Liquid Detergent

Laundry Liquid Detergent
Bio-D (biod.co.uk)
Miniml (minimlrefills.co.uk)
Ecover (uk.ecover.com) and in most supermarkets

Marseille Soap Stain Bar
For a Cheval Marseille Stain Remover Bar (with ridges; www.frenchsoaps.co.uk)

Netted Soap Either make one of these from the recycled plastic netting
around citrus fruit, or use a soap bar with ridges made for friction – see note
for Marseille soap

Oxygen Bleach (Sodium Percarbonate, 100%)
Allavare (allavare.co.uk)

French Soaps (www.frenchsoaps.co.uk)
Mistral Cleaning Products (mistralie.co.uk)
Peace With The Wild (peacewiththewild.co.uk)
&Keep (andkeep.com)

Pheromone Traps
Dragonfli (dragonfli.co.uk)

Reed Diffusers & Bases
Augeo Diffuser Base (thesoapkitchen.co.uk) (candle-shack.co.uk)

Rubber Gloves
Seep (theseepcompany.com)

Rubbing Alcohol (Isopropanol IPA 70%)
Hexeal (hexeal.co.uk)
Ican London (icanlondon.com)

Soap bars – see Stain Removal Soap Bar

Soda Crystals
Dri-Pak (dri-pak.co.uk) – see note for Bicarb

Soda Crystals Liquid – see note for Bicarb

Stain Removal Soap Bar
For a Cheval Marseille Stain Remover Bar (with ridges; www.frenchsoaps.co.uk)
La Maison Du Savon de Marseille Stain Remover Stick
(maison-du-savon-de-Marseille.fr)
Re:gn Natural Stain Remover Soap (with ridges; regn.co.uk)
Bette's Stain Bar (allavare.co.uk).
Bio-D Laundry & Stain Remover Bar (biggreensmile.com)
Soap Nuts Natural Stain Removal Bar (soapnuts.co.uk)

Washing-up Liquid
Bio-D (biod.co.uk)
Bower Collective (bowercollective.com)
Ecoleaf (suma-store.coop)
Ecover (uk.ecover.com) and available in most supermarkets

Water Hardness Test Strips
Scalemaster (diy.com)

White Vinegar (5%)
Big Green Smile (biggreensmile.com)
Robert Dyas (robertdyas.co.uk)
Hexeal (hexeal.co.uk)
Harbour Housewares 5L (rinkit.com)

INDEX

ACKNOWLEDGEMENTS

A huge thank you to our editor Katie Law, without whom this book would not have seen the light of day. Katie was our 'lightning rod' and always found a way through sticky patches. We are so grateful to her for her remarkable skill in working between the two of us and keeping us both happy and on track.

A special thanks to our publishers Aurea Carpenter and Rebecca Nicolson, who saw the point of this book right away and have encouraged us and shaped our thinking to the final full stop. Louise Atkinson who attended a workshop in the early days and helped with editing.

Huge thanks to our chemists Anna Slastanova and Margaret Karlinski who went far beyond the call of duty and read several drafts of this book well into the night. James Wood, who has been through every stain and every draft of this book from the very beginning and seen Purdy through all the tech wizardry needed with the utmost patience and humour.

Jennie Morris and Josephine Marchendise who came to our very first workshop in the garage, which we held just for the two of them. They have been encouraging us ever since.

Thank you to all the friends who have relentlessly supported us over the years, the people who came to our workshops in the garage and the friends who hosted often more than one workshop in their homes: Yvonna Demczyuska, Ravida Clay, Marianne de Giorgio, Mary James, Rebecca Law, Katie Naylor, Marie-Helene Oliver, Celia Prideaux, Sarah Spence.

Gary Haynes and Jack Duell (ready for anything from day one in the garage), Archie Figg (our Stain Squad hero), Catherine Alliott, Anna Bagnall, Jane Bryden Brown , Danny Danziger, Nicola Glucksmann, Heather Jackson, Stephen and Adele Martin, Donna Nathan, Mary Villiers. Chris Buzzard, plumbing engineer Suffolk. Bryan Williams, Premiere Appliance Servicing, Bedfordshire. Carolyn Flook, The Natural Laundry, Amersham.

To Purdy's sons Charlie and Jack Rubin, who have grown Purdy and Figg from a dream in a garage to the business it is today.

And, finally, our husbands Stephen Rubin and Christopher Figg, who never complained when our homes were turned into kitchen-chemistry labs or when they came home from work to find the house doubling up as a launderette. Most of all, they have been a constant source of encouragement and laughs.

ABOUT THE AUTHORS

Purdy Rubin is the co-founder of Purdy & Figg. After working at Christies, London, and then setting up the Purdy Hicks Gallery in 1987 (formerly Pomeroy Purdy), she studied homeopathy and went on to train as a nurse, working at the Michael Sobell Hospice at Mount Vernon. With Charlotte Figg, she studied Essential Oils and Soap Making at the Middlesex School of Complementary Medicine with Margaret Karlinski before setting up their company together with her two sons, Charlie and Jack, in 2020. She lives in Suffolk and is married with four grown-up children.

Before co-founding Purdy & Figg, **Charlotte Figg** worked on board-level strategy projects for Barclays Bank, Sainsbury's, B&Q and Superdrug. She has conducted customer-research projects in the UK and US for companies and charities including Boden, Crocus and Pret à Manger, and in 2017 set up the Crocus Garden School. She lives in Buckinghamshire with her husband and has three grown-up children.

This is their first book.

Published in 2025 by New River Books
Unit 105, Leroy House, 436 Essex Road, London N1 3QP
www.newriverbooks.co.uk

10 9 8 7 6 5 4 3 2 1

A CIP catalogue record for this book is available from the British Library.

ISBN: 978-1-915780-44-7

Cover and interior design by Smith & Gilmour
Cover and interior illustrations by Chiara Perano
Editor: Judy Barratt
Consultant writer: Louise Atkinson

Printed and Bound in the UK using 100% Renewable Electricity at
CPI Group (UK) Ltd, Croydon, CRO 4YY.
This FSC© label means that materials used for the product have been responsibly sourced.

MIX
Paper | Supporting
responsible forestry
FSC® C013604

Where images or quotes have been used in this text, every effort has been made
to contact copyright holders and abide by 'fair use' guidelines. If you are a copyright
holder and wish to get in touch, please email info@newriverbooks.co.uk

DISCLAIMER

The information provided in this book is for educational purposes only and is not
intended to be a substitute for professional advice. The authors are not liable for any
damage, injury or loss that may result from the use of the natural cleaning products
described. Readers are advised to always use caution and test products in a small area
before wider application. By using the recipes and tips in this book, readers assume
all risks associated with the use of the ingredients involved.

Additionally, on essential oils: never use these undiluted or internally unless advised
by your health provider or certified aromatherapist. Keep essential oils away from infants,
children and pets. If pregnant or breastfeeding, consult with your healthcare provider
or a certified aromatherapist before using any essential oils. We do not use, promote
or recommend the use of essential oils from endangered sources.